Single & Complete

- ABRAHAM A JONES -

Cover design by Maestro Creative

Typeset in the United Kingdom by
PrintOnDemand-Worldwide

 Benorah
Publications

Dedication

This book is dedicated to my precious son, Josh and to all the single men and women across the world.

Acknowledgments

To my heavenly Father; it is a privilege to call you "Father". To my earthly parents; I am proud and honoured to be your son.

I want to appreciate my lovely wife, Ashma and my precious son, Joshua for their love and support.

I also want to acknowledge Peter and Daniel Jones for inspiring me in many ways. A big "thank you" to all my brothers and sisters, I love you all.

To the crewmembers of the Life Singles Network and Kingdom Relationships, may God bless you beyond measure.

To everyone who has encouraged me in anyway over the years, may God's face shine on you!

Contents

Introduction

God did not design us as incomplete beings or institute marriage in order to make us feel complete.

Relationships and marriage consist of a man and a woman, two different individuals, coming together on the basis of true love as one flesh. What these individuals know and do can go a very long way to determine how well or poorly things turn out for them. Unfortunately, many people blame everything but themselves for the failure of their relationships. They play the blame-game, thinking it would make them feel better. But, it does not.

What you know and how you live your life before you go into a relationship can determine whether you will be an asset or a liability to the person you will eventually go into a serious relationship with. Many singles rush into marriage in order to escape singleness because they do not know the purpose of singleness. They think that by being in a relationship, their life will be complete.

God's desire and plan for those who are single is for them to step into a relationship or marriage "complete" and "whole" as a person. It was never God's plan to use marriage to complete His children. Many relationships and marriages are failing today because people go into a relationship expecting the other party to give them a sense of completeness and wholeness. They later become frustrated when they are unable to achieve this expectation.

I often tell single people that if they do not know how to be single and happy, they may find it hard to be happy in a marriage. So many singles put their dreams, careers and life on hold because they want to be in a relationship or marriage. It is not a wise thing to do.

A single man or woman that understands singleness will not be ashamed or uncomfortable with his or her single life. Singleness is not a stigma; it is, rather, a phase of life to be lived and enjoyed to the full.

God's plan is for you to enjoy the single phase of your life and maximize it. This book will show you what singleness is, how to enjoy it, and what you need to know before and during relationships. It will explore some deep questions that you need to ask yourself before and during your relationship. It will look into God's plan for and many things that would prepare and equip you for a successful relationship.

This book is a must-read for every single-person who wants to enjoy their singleness, relationship, marriage and life. Do not go into a relationship unprepared. Successful relationships and marriages don't happen by accident; they are built by people who prepared and equipped themselves beforehand.

The best time to prepare for a relationship is before you go into one. The best time to prepare is now. Read and discover truths about singleness and how to enjoy and make the most of it. Singleness is not a curse; it is a blessing. It is a phase of life that needs to be enjoyed and not just endured.

Abraham A Jones

Section 1

Chapter One
Singleness

Being single is a gift God freely gave everyone regardless of their race, gender or religion. You will be robbing yourself a great deal if you fail to recognize and enjoy this natural gift of being single. Even if you were born a twin, you have the right to enjoy your singleness. In this book, I will address two types of singleness. These are what I call: *1) Relational Singleness, 2) Intrinsic Singleness.* We will consider the first type in this chapter and the second later.

Relational Singleness is when someone is unmarried. In other words, they are not in a marriage relationship with another person. A number of people fall under this category, including those who have never been married, people who were once married and are now divorced, single parents, widows and widowers.

A season of *Relational Singleness* is the time you spend on your own before you commit to a relationship or marriage; it is a phase in the lives of people, especially for people who intend to get married someday.

Nobody was born married, and the time you spend on your own before you commit to a marriage relationship is your season of relational singleness.

The importance of your single days cannot be over-emphasized. They are your valuable years of self-discovery and exploration.

The duration people spend in their relational single days differs from person to person. Some spend less time than others. The bottom line, however, is that everyone goes through this phase of life. No matter how long it lasts, Relational Singleness is meant to end when we commit to a marriage relationship.

Unfortunately, many people get married and still live their lives in a state of relational singleness!

This is very dangerous for any relationship because, it can make parties to such a relationship feel estranged to each other though married. The last thing anyone wants is to be married to someone who still acts and lives his or her life as a single person. This is the reason why many are married but lonely.

Some get too used to living an independent and single life and they find it hard to adjust even after marrying someone they love. It can be difficult to adjust especially if you have stayed a bit longer in the relational single phase of life. In as much as it is vital to enjoy your relational single life, it is equally important to consciously make adjustments when the time comes for you to marry.

When you find love and plan to get married, you should happily make adjustments no matter how difficult it may be in order to accommodate the new person that is about to come into your life. A major reason people give for their divorces is "irreconcilable differences", which is the result of people failing to make the necessary changes in certain areas of their life.

As a single person, when you are ready to marry, the first thing you should consciously address is how to practically put an end to relational singleness. Begin to imagine and plan how you will share your life on a daily basis with someone else. Generally, this should be easy if the person is someone you love.

Failure to know when and how to put an end to the relational singleness mentality can ruin a marriage relationship. We will take a look at intrinsic singleness later in the book.

SINGLE AND COMPLETE

"...and the two shall become one flesh." Matt 19:5.

The above statement was made by our Lord Jesus Christ in a bid to enlighten the religious leaders of His day. It is very important to note that Jesus said, "...and the two..." He was making reference to two, separate, whole and complete individuals who decided to come together as one in Holy matrimony.

As a single person, it is imperative that you live life as a whole individual before walking down the aisle with someone else. A lot of people step into relationships and eventually marriages as incomplete individuals seeking someone else to make them complete. This eventually leads to marriages where parties involved become emotionally, psychologically and spiritually drained, because one or both parties came into the relationship half-a-person, expecting only to receive.

Learning to deal with issues that make you feel less as a person before getting married is critical; failure to do this will give you a wrong impression about marriage and make relating with a spouse very difficult and complicated.

Before Eve came into Adam's life, Adam had a life. He was complete and whole, doing what his boss (God) would have him do. Eve was classified as a "helper". She also came into the scene complete, so much so that Adam could not hide his feelings from her.

Ladies! Do you want to be respected by your future man? Then, step into his life complete! The same goes for the guys. Many men and women walk into marriages hoping to find the father or mother they never had. Some come in looking for the luxury they never had as kids. Genesis 2:18: "And the Lord said, it is not good that the man should be alone; I will make a help mate for him."

The above scripture has often been misinterpreted. So many people think Eve was created to complete Adam. That was not the case. Eve was not created because Adam was incomplete. Rather, she was created to complement Adam. Adam was created complete and whole, and so was Eve. The moment you start feeling like you need a man or a woman to be complete in life, it is a clear indication that you have been misinformed or you have misconceptions about your completeness.

Our God is a complete God. He is all-knowing, all-powerful and He does not create incomplete things. We are created in God's image and likeness and since there is no trace of incompleteness in Him, we have no business with incompleteness. It is the enemy that lies to so many people using different things and circumstances to make people feel incomplete and insecure. Colossians 2: 9-10 says: "For in Him dwells all the fullness of the Godhead bodily; [10] and you are complete in Him, who is the head of all principality and power." If you are not satisfied as a single person, marriage on its own will not satisfy you. I have heard a lot of people say that when they get married, their depression, anger, insecurity, etc. will be gone. What a lie! This kind of mindset is a set-up for future disappointment. It is important you deal with these issues before leaving the single's territory. A depressed, angry or frustrated single man or woman will definitely be a depressed, angry and frustrated man or woman when married.

Look at yourself the way God sees you and be the best you can be in order to earn the respect that comes with wholeness as a single person.

The best your spouse, or future spouse, can and should do is to complement you. The moment you expect them to make you feel complete; you are making a huge mistake.

Are you single and in a relationship? Don't get too excited when your spouse tells you he or she is incomplete without you. If they do, you should ask, "How do you mean?" Failure to address these issues may leave one or both parties emotionally, physically, spiritually, financially or mentally drained in a relationship.

Chapter Two

Transformers & Amplifiers

To transform a thing simply means to change it from one form to another. It also means to transfigure or convert the function or structure of a thing from what it used to be to something different. Amplifiers on the other hand are devices used to increase the power of already existing signals.

Many couples have gone into relationships and eventually marriages with the wrong assumption that marriage on its own will bring about a transformation or a transfiguration in their attitude or character. This is not true at all. The truth of the matter is that marriage will not transform your character; it will only amplify it.

You may pretend to be who you are not in the early stages of a relationship, but after a while your true character and identity will begin to unfold. Even if you pretend while dating or courting someone, it will become very difficult to keep on pretending in marriage. The real you will manifest in time.

After a few months or years of marriage, some begin to complain that their spouse's character changed. However, upon investigation, they will discover that in fact, this was how they were all along. If you fail to improve on your attitude or deal with crucial character flaws, you may end up

15

destroying your future marriage with your own hands. When it comes to attitude and character, marriage is an amplifier and not a transformer.

Marriage has a way of amplifying your strengths and weaknesses over time. As a single person, do not overlook an attitude or habit that needs correction, because it might cost you a lot later. It is easier, relatively speaking, to deal with a bad habit while single than when married. As a married person, that bad habit will not just affect you; it will also affect your family, directly or indirectly.

Going into a relationship or marriage, therefore, with a bad habit is like turning the volume of a sound system to the highest level even when what is playing is detestable. Due to the many twist and turns in marriage, a time will come when who you really are will begin to reflect no matter how hard you try to suppress it.

Years ago, a friend introduced me to a lady he just got into a relationship with. He was serious about the relationship and planned to marry her. There was no doubt that he loved her and I could see in her eyes that she was really in love and happy with him.

He told me with much excitement how they met in Church and how she loves God etc. However, a few months into the relationship, he started noticing some red flags that questioned her character and faithfulness. He thought he was being insecure and decided to overlook them.

After a while, as the relationship and marriage preparation got more serious, it became obvious that this lady was having affairs with a number of people. My friend was heartbroken and his question was, "Why?" He loved her and had everything she could want. Besides, she 'loved' him too.

Upon investigation, it was discovered that commitment to one relationship at a time had always been a struggle for her. Although she really wanted to have a family with this guy and did not want to lose him, she lost out on the promising relationship because of her ongoing problem. She did not deal with her bad habit and as a result forfeited a potentially decent relationship.

If you fail to deal with a character flaw, it may end up dealing with you and costing you a whole lot in the future.

The lady was heartbroken and disappointed when the guy called the relationship off. If she had worked on her issues earlier, it would have been a different story for her today.

The best time to improve on your character is while you are still single. Examine yourself and ask yourself a few honest questions: Have I got a bad attitude that can put my future husband or wife off? Have I got issues with uncontrollable rage, telling lies, unfaithfulness, etc.?

If you identify any undesirable trait, do not sweep it under the carpet. Deal with it; seek help; look for books and people who can help you overcome the bad habit.

I met another single lady some time back in the United Kingdom. She really loved the Lord and was very committed to her local church. But she had issues with uncontrollable anger. One minute she was like an angel serving in God's house, and the next minute she would react and shout the whole place down when someone said something she did not like.

Her dedication and passion for God attracted people to her, including potential suitors, but after a while, when they witnessed a few displays of her uncontrollable rage, they vanished into thin air and maintained their distance.

She wondered why suitors refused to stay around. People and friends were scared to point out the obvious to her; they did not want to partake of her outbursts.

One day, she opened up and told me how she was disappointed many times by people who promised to marry her but did not keep to their word. I listened attentively as she painted a picture, describing herself as the victim. In the process of counselling, I told her about my observation and the need for her to improve on her character as it would be good for her, and better her chances of meeting her potential husband. She listened attentively and took the advice I gave her.

The next time I saw her, she was so excited to tell me that though it was not easy for her to deal with the anger, she succeeded with the help of the Holy Spirit, and subsequently she met a very good man. For the first time in her life, she was in a very serious relationship and they are already planning their wedding. I was happy for her and advised her to keep improving on herself because she would be tested even in marriage.

The best person that can transform you is *you*, with the help of God of course – if you let Him work in and through you. Be honest with yourself and with God; open up yourself for Him to touch and transform any aspect of your life that needs transformation while you are still single. Do not wait until you are married before you work on your deficiencies; deal with then now!

If you think marriage will transform your bad attitudes to good attitudes, you are sadly mistaken. Marriage will only increase the volume of your attitude over time.

This does not mean that you cannot improve on your character when you are married; of course you can and should. However, it would be a lot easier to deal with crucial character deficiencies before you involve yourself in a marriage relationship.

The scriptures says in *Rom 12:2: "And be not conformed to this world; but be ye transformed by the renewing of your mind, that ye may prove what is that good, acceptable and perfect will of God".*

The above verse makes us understand that true and lasting transformation takes place within us, in our mind and spirit. A reformed mind is a transformed mind and if your mind is transformed, it affects every aspect of your life.

The human mind is a subdivision of the human soul. The human soul is a vital aspect of every human being, comprising of our mind, will and emotions. It is a very powerful tool that can take you to limitless heights if properly utilized. The mistake many people make is that they try so hard to change externally at the expense of internal change.

The change of clothes, jobs, geographical location or marital status does not transform a man; true transformation is the one that is effected from within the man via his mind. With our minds we imagine, think, create and carry out many other functions. This is why I believe that whatever controls and dominates your mind will eventually control and dominate you. Rid yourself of ideas, thoughts, imaginations and mindsets that hinder you from being who God originally designed you to be.

Feed your mind and transform your person with positive things, and use the word of God to saturate your mind so it can be subject to the Holy Spirit.

The latter part of Romans 12:2 clearly makes us understand that in order for us to be able to substantiate the good, acceptable and perfect will of God, our mind needs to be renewed first. Do you want to experience a better life? Do you want to make the most of your God-given life? Do you want to avoid destroying your relationships and future with your own hands, like many people do? If your answer is "yes", then, renew your mind!

When we renew our minds, we experience transformation in every aspect of our lives, especially in our relationships with people.

The Odyssey of Character

Your skills, education, wealth, gifts, beauty or charm may elevate and expose you to greatness, however, what will determine how long and how well you remain on top is your character. Your character is what people really know you by. The impression we leave in people's lives during and after our time on earth is mainly reflected via our character.

Your character is the sum total of the person you are. It contains and reflects your traits, morals, ethics, etc. Your character reflects your true identity. However, your character does not just happen to you; it is formed over time. There are processes involved in the stages that eventually metamorphose into someone's character.

Let us take a quick look at the journey of character from the nine important stages of character-formation and direction in everyone's life. I will skip the first stage for now and go straight to the second stage:

Stage 2> **Your Thoughts:**~ What goes on in your mind plays a major role in your character formation. The thoughts that go through your mind will, over time, be reflected in your character. It is very important to filter the thoughts that go through your mind. An unhealthy thought may randomly come to your mind, but you can decide to meditate on it or swiftly get it out of your mind.

A lot of people allow negative thoughts to remain in their minds and after a while, they begin to brood on them. Before they know it, the negative thoughts will be hatched around them. Beware of what you let into your mind and most importantly, of how long you allow a negative thought to remain in your mind.

Your mind is a major gate into your life and what you allow in via the gate may over time dominate your life. Many people have allowed negative thoughts to build strongholds in their lives – strongholds that eventually hold them captive in life. Whatever dominates your mind will eventually dominate your life. No wonder the scripture says in Proverbs 23:7: "As he thinks in his heart, so is he..." Show me the content of a man's mind and I will tell you what controls his life.

Positive thoughts create a positive life and negative thoughts will negatively affect a person's life. Saturate your mind with positive thoughts and your life will eventually be surrounded by positive things. If your mind is under attack by negative thoughts, apply 2 Corinthians 10:5 and you will have victory in your thought life. Stage 3> **Your Words**:~ Your thoughts go a very long way to determine what comes out of your mouth. The scripture says in Proverbs 18:21: "...death and life are in the power of the tongue: and they that love it shall eat the fruit thereof." The things you say will eventually frame your life, and the things you say once existed as thoughts in your mind.

I believe that there is no such thing as a "slip of the tongue" because, each word that comes out of our mouths was first formed in our mind. I see so many people who, in a moment of anger, say all kinds of things to the person or persons they are angry with, only to come back later and say they did not mean what they said, or cannot remember saying them.

It is very crucial that we monitor and filter our thoughts because they will in turn determine our words; and our words say a lot about us.

One of the best ways to get to know people is by having conversations with them. A simple chat with someone can tell a lot about that person. Relationships are built through communication and a significant percentage of communication is verbal. However, many people missed out on great relationships and opportunities because of what came out of their lips.

A young man saw a lady he really liked and after weeks of preparation he decided to approach her for a serious relationship. On the fateful day he decided to make his move. He got his appearance right; he was nicely and smartly dressed. His appearance was appealing to the lady when he approached her after the church service. He offered to walk her to her car and in the process he intended to make his move by telling her how he felt about her. Unfortunately, things did not work out as he intended.

He succeeded in getting her attention, but when the time came for him to say something, the "wrong" words came out of his mouth. When he opened his mouth, he was carried away by the dirty thoughts he had been having about her and before he realized it, his mouth was pouring them out. The lady felt embarrassed and angrily ended the conversation.

He tried to apologize subsequently, but it was already too late. This is just an example of the dangers of using the wrong words as a result of allowing the wrong thoughts into our minds. Many people have missed out on great business opportunities in life because of the content of their words.

Some singles are unable to converse without swearing, cursing or saying something that may put decent people off. As a result, people avoid them whenever they can.

Many marriages have ended because of the poor use of words by one or both parties in the marriage. The scripture says in Matthew 12:37: "For by your words you will be justified, and by your words you will be condemned."

Having control over your tongue will preserve your life and open great doors for you.

Be mindful of what comes out of your mouth as a single person because it goes a long way to leaving a lasting impression on people's minds about you. Filter the thoughts that go through your mind and you will worry less about the content of your words.

Stage 4> **Your Emotions**:~ Your emotions are an aspect of your soul; they are the conscious part of you through which fear, joy, love, hate, sorrow, anger etc are experienced and expressed.

Your thoughts and words shape your emotions. Your mood, your temperaments and the things that motivate you in life are all functions of your emotions.

God gave us emotions so we could express ourselves better and communicate on a deeper level, which is why we sometimes show healthy emotions when we love, worship or pray. Unfortunately, many people are held captive emotionally as a result of their thoughts and the words that come out of their mouths. Issues like depression, obsession, anxiety, low self-esteem and fear are emotional strongholds that hold many people captive.

Feed your mind with positive things and your words will be full of life; and in addition to that, your emotions will be healthy. However, if you are going through emotional issues like depression, anxiety and low self-esteem, there is nothing to be ashamed of. Seek help from God and from professionals in order to better your life and maximize your potentials. Regardless of your current state emotionally, you can transform your life for the better by improving the content of your mind.

The greatest battles in life are fought in the mind. If you can invest positively in yours, you are on your way to a successful life; and one of the best ways to develop and renew your mind is by meditating on, believing in and obeying the word of God. Regardless of your current mental state, God can turn your life around if you believe and reach out to His outstretched arm.

Failure to deal with emotional problems before marriage may result in complications in relationships leading to marriage and during marriage. I have come across so many single people, who struggled with low self-esteem, depression, fear, etc., but they decided to surrender it all to God at the cross and He came to their rescue before they got into serious relationships. On the other hand, some people went into serious relationships and marriage with unresolved issues and these complicated their lives in the long run.

Before you jump into a relationship, search yourself to see if there are areas that need renewing or improving. By so doing, you will be positively investing in your life and future.

Stage 5> **Your Decisions**:~ One of the greatest gifts and abilities that humans have is the ability to make decisions. Your decisions are engineered by your will and your will is an aspect of your soul – the instrument through which decisions are made or refused to be made. The quality of your decisions in life will determine the quality of your future. Many people have wasted many years of their lives because of wrong decisions they made earlier in life.

The things that inform our decisions in life revolve around our thoughts, words and emotions, hence the need to filter what we allow in and around us.

As a single person, one of the greatest decisions you will ever make in life is deciding who to marry. This decision can make or break you. Poor decisions are the result of poor judgment and poor judgments are the result of inadequate information. This explains why so many people have ended up in bad relationships. The person you decide to marry can determine whether you will live a happy or sad life. Do not leave your life to chance or indecision. After all, indecision is a decision not to make a decision.

To improve on the quality of your decisions is to improve your life. Do not live your life passively. Rather, live consciously and actively, understanding the above stages, and you will notice a remarkable difference in your life.

Since our decisions can determine how the future turns out for us, it is very important that we do not make crucial decisions hastily or angrily. Do not allow your emotions alone to dictate to you. Get information. Reason and meditate before you make these decisions. Always remember that every decision you make has either a positive or a negative consequence.

As a believer, the Holy Spirit is the best Guide when it comes to making decisions. The knowledge of the Holy Spirit is limitless and the depth of His understanding is endless. You cannot get it wrong with His guidance. As good and as ever-present as God's spirit is, many people ignore Him even when they are about to make crucial decisions. The scripture says in Proverbs 3:5-6: "Trust in the Lord with all your heart; and lean not unto your own understanding. In all thy ways acknowledge him, and he shall direct your paths."

Regardless of your level of intelligence, experience and education, your decisions without the Holy Spirit are porous; Spirit-influenced decisions are superior and more reliable than ordinary decisions.

Stage 6> **Your Actions:**~ Your actions are steps you take in order to execute your decisions. Our actions in life are mainly propelled by the decisions we have already made within us. Before we make a move to do something, the decision is made first and the next thing that follows is a corresponding act that reflects the decision we have made. For example, if you run out of milk, bread or cheese at home, the next thing you do is decide when and where to buy more. When that time comes, you wilfully move out of the house to the grocery store.

Going to the grocery store is the action you have taken as a result of the decision you made, which also stemmed from the thought you had about the need to get more milk, bread or cheese.

Your actions, therefore, reflect how you think and the decisions you make. Good decisions give birth to good actions and bad decisions give birth to bad actions.

Are you always disappointed by the things you do? Are your actions setting you back? Do people around you complain about your actions? If your answer is "yes" to any of these, then there is a need to improve on the quality of the decisions you make.

It is very important we evaluate our actions because they do not just affect our today; they also affect our future. They are like seeds that we sow and reap over time. Walking into a serious relationship, investing in a business venture, buying a house, etc., are actions we take with futuristic consequences. The Bible paints a clear picture in Galatians 6:7: "Be not deceived; God is not mocked: for whatever a man sows, that shall he also reap."

Be very mindful of your actions because they go a long way to determine the kind of future that awaits you. Involve God in your decision-making process and evaluate your actions in the light of His words; and with time, you will be stepping into a glorious future.

Stage 7> **Your Habits**:~ Your habits are the behavioural patterns you adopt and follow over time until they become part of you. You get so used to these behavioural patterns that you unconsciously get accustomed to them.

Some people have the habit of bathing twice a day, having a cup of tea before going to bed at night, cleaning their homes every Saturday, etc. We all have habits and most times, we don't even take note of them as much as the people around us do.

The actions we carry out over time eventually become our habits. In other words, good actions will translate into good habits and bad actions will translate into bad habits. The salient thing about habits is that when we get used to them, we begin to practice them involuntarily.

Habits take time to build, but once formed, they are very difficult to get rid of. That is why it is very important to watch and manage your actions, or else you might get stuck to habits that are destructive.

I have come across so many people who feel imprisoned by their habits. Serious issues like drug addiction and alcohol addiction start in subtle ways; and over time, the people involved become so attached to these ways to the point that they become habits.

Bad habits are strongholds that can destroy relationships and marriages. As a single person, you might have acquired some bad habits over time; it is vital, then, that you search yourself thoroughly before you get married. When you get married, your habits, both good and bad are amplified, and when they become amplified, it is your spouse that will either benefit from them or get victimized by them.

The last thing you want to do is to hurt the person you love; unfortunately, many lovers hurt themselves unconsciously, because their habits have become a negative stronghold in their lives.

Have you got a bad habit that sets you back and brings you shame and embarrassment? Don't cover it up. Seek help and deal with it. Don't be comfortable with a bad habit; failure to work on your bad habits might cost you a lot in the future. Many people work so hard to get to the top of their careers, businesses, ministries and endeavours only to come crashing down because of a bad habit that has come to light.

Do not wait for your bad habit to destroy, dent or defame you before you tackle it. The more time you give your bad habit, the more roots it develops within you, and the more roots your bad habits has in you, the stronger the hold it will have over you.

There is a scripture I always love sharing with people who are willing to seek help with a bad habit. It is found in Romans 7:15: "For what I am doing, I do not understand. For what I will to do, that I do not practice; but what I hate, that I do." This scripture paints the picture of so many people's lives.

They desire so much to do good, but their bad habits have a stronghold over them to the point where they are seemingly helpless. The good news is that God can deliver you from any kind of stronghold if you allow Him to step into the situation. I have seen God deliver people from bad habits that once held them captive. For with God, all things are possible!

Stage 8> **Your Character:**~ Your character is your true identity and as we have seen so far, it undergoes many processes before it is formed: your thoughts, words, emotions, decisions, actions and habits equal your character. What your colleagues, friends and family will remember you by when you are long gone is resident in your character. Just like the scripture says in Matthew 7:16: "You shall know them by their fruits. Do men gather grapes from thorns, or figs from thistles?"

Just as a mango tree does not produce guava fruits, but only mangoes, good habits produce good character and bad habits produce bad character. You may try so hard to hide a bad character, but eventually, like smoke, it will come out for all to see. The same applies to persons with good character. You may be in the most obscure places on the planet, but if you have a good character, it will speak well of you even long after you are gone.

Your wealth, connections, skills and talents cannot take the place of your character. Over time, people around you will be able to distinguish between what you have and the person you really are. People with a bad character may pretend to be good, but all it will take is time for their real self to manifest. As a single person, even if you succeed in hiding your true character, when you get married your spouse will eventually decode who you really are.

Many people are well respected by people from afar, but the people closest to them have no regard for them because they know who they really are. One of the most difficult roles to play in this life is the role of a hypocrite. Pretending to be someone that you are not will not just cost you, it will also cost the people closest to you. Many relationships and marriages are broken today because one or both parties pretended to be someone they were not; they tried to conceal their true identity until they could do so no longer. You can only pretend for so long; after a while, your real fruits will begin to blossom for all to see.

What do you want people to remember you by? How do you want to be remembered? Even if you are a philanthropist and you have a bad character, when you are long gone, people will not just remember you for what you did for them, they will also remember you for the person you really were. The time to improve on your character is now. Do not wait until it is too late, what you need to do is make a genuine decision to change and let God step into your life.

In the book of Matthew Chapter 19 from verses 1-10, we see how a man by the name of Zacchaeus, who had a very bad reputation, habit and character, made a decision to change. He allowed Jesus into his life to effect the change. His life was transformed when he encountered Christ and he started bearing good fruits evident for all to see. The people he cheated, extorted and defrauded were reimbursed double. God can do the same for you if you really want to change and if you allow Him into your life. If God can do it for Zaccheaus and many others, He can do it for you.

Your character is not an end in itself; it is a pathway that leads somewhere. Let us take a look at another stage, a stage mainly determined by our character:

Stage 9> **Your Destination**:~ So far we have seen the journey involved in character formation and how important each stage involved in our character formation is. The truth of the matter is that your character can determine where you are heading in life. An average person desires a good future and hopes for a better life, but unfortunately, it is not enough to desire a good future and it is not even enough to have great plans and strategies, you need more than that, you need the right character to complement your hope, desires and plans.

Many people have been deceived into believing that their destiny is something that they have little or no say in. Though our future is in God's hands and He is able to do all things, we have a major role to play in fully realizing it.

He desires the best for us as His children and has made great provisions for us in the realm of the Spirit. However, just because provisions have been made already does not mean that everyone is going to access them. Our character, habits, actions, decisions, emotions, words and thoughts can determine if we step into our glorious future or not.

Are you single? God has already prepared your dream partner, family and home, but in order for you to experience these things, there is a role you have to play. For instance, just because someone decides to pay for your dream holiday in the Bahamas, Hawaii or the Maldives does not mean that you have no role to play in getting there. Though the trip has been paid for, you still need to show up at the airport at the right time and check into the hotel or resort at the stipulated time. Failure to do all these may cause you to forfeit the trip.

The same applies to life. Just because you are hopeful, positive, full of faith and lofty plans does not mean that everything is going to fall in place. You will still need to take the right steps in the right direction in order to get to your destination. Where you are today is the result of your previous thoughts, words, emotions, decisions, actions, habits and character. Where you desire to be tomorrow will also be determined by the words, thoughts, emotions, decisions, actions, habits and character that you exhibit today.

I met a single lady some years ago in the city of London who said God showed her a glimpse of her future husband and kids, as well as the geographical location they were going to live. Shortly afterwards she met a guy who fitted perfectly the revelation she had. The moment they met, they became friends. She was so excited.

She assumed though, that every other thing that was revealed to her was going to manifest. As months went by, she became so relaxed and began to take undue advantage of this guy. She would not show up for appointments, dates and other planned engagements. She would travel and leave town without even letting him know. She assumed it was going to work out anyhow, anyway.

After a while, the guy became discouraged and though he loved her so much, he felt she did not love him half as much as he did, and as a result, he called off the relationship. She could not believe her ears. She wept and lamented but it was too late. She failed to understand that she had a role to play in bringing the revealed future into reality.

31

As a single person, you need to understand the fact that your character can determine whether you will get into your desired destination in life or not. Do not wait until you are married; it might complicate your relationship then. The best time to start working and improving on your character is now. Wise singles prepare ahead of time. What you do today will determine your destination tomorrow.

Let us now look at the first stage that I intentionally left until now. This stage is so vital and important that it can control all the above stages:

Stage 1> **Influence**;~ Every human being on earth is a product of influence. Our thoughts, words, emotions, decisions, actions, habits, character and destination in life are shaped by the things that influence us. The things we do in life and the reasons we do them are as a result of the forces that influences our lives. The people, things, sights and sounds we are exposed to over time become a strong force that influence our belief and value systems.

This influence begins the moment we come into the world. The family your are born into, the environment you grow up in, the things and way you learn in school, the books you read, the things you see, the things you hear, etc. are all strong forces that influence your life in one way or the other.

As babies or little children, we have little or no control over these avenues of influence. However, when we grow into adults, it becomes our responsibility to have control over what we allow to influence our lives. The people that speak into your life can either put fear or confidence into you.

I met a lady several years ago in England. Although she was a beautiful and intelligent believer, she had phobia for marriage. She was so negative about marriage, relationships, couples and anything that reflected love. I was so concerned.

We got talking one day and after a lengthy conversation, I discovered that her perception on relationships and love was influenced by her immediate environment.

Her father treated her mother badly when she was growing up. She was abused as a child and most of her family members experienced the same thing. As a result, there was so much resentment and negative perception about relationships, love and marriage. This negative influence held her bound for years until she encountered God's love in a mighty way and the siege over her life was broken.

I encouraged her to filter what she allows into her ears, and to learn from people who have successful relationships and marriages. She took the counsel and surrounded herself with believers who encouraged her in the things of God. Before long, they became a strong and positive influence over her life. She read books, went to seminars and conferences that spoke life into her. To the glory of God, it paid off, and today she is happily married to a man she loves and who loves her. She now believes in love so much and counsels others who are where she used to be years ago.

Are you struggling or suffering as a result of the effects of the negative influences in your life? The same God that did it for that lady can do the same and even much more in your life.

Although, we are influenced by various things and people around us, we are also instruments of influence in the lives of those in our life. The things we do and say directly or indirectly influence others. This understanding will make us mindful of the things we say and do.

Choose to be a positive influence in someone's life today.

In today's world, one of the greatest influences in young people's lives is the media. You, therefore, need to be very careful not to absorb everything the media pushes on you. The lyrics of the songs you listen to, the kind of movies you watch, the type of books you read and the kind of people you hang around will go a very long way to determine the thoughts that come to your mind– your thoughts will give birth to your words; your words will then shape your emotions; your emotions will in turn determine your decisions; your decisions equals your habits; your habits define your character; and your character will eventually determine your destination in life.

Chapter Three

Singleness is not a Disease

The way singleness is portrayed by many today is really disturbing. Some people feel as if singleness is a form of disease. The media has not helped matters at all. the notion sold by the media that sex is a must-do activity and that having multiple sexual partners is normal, has gradually been accepted by many people. As a result, many cannot imagine being single.

Singleness is one of the major seasons in our lives, and we should cherish it while it lasts. Desperation to be in a relationship or to get married has landed so many people in places they least expected to be. A Broken heart, shattered dreams, disappointments, pain and **scars** are what many are left with today, just because they were in a hurry to be in a relationship. One of the major reasons why the divorce rate is skyrocketing today is that most people jump into marriages for the wrong reasons.

Sometime ago, I met a lady who was in such a hurry to get married because most of her friends were either married or planning to get married. I counselled her to be patient and to make the most of her life by focusing on other aspects of life before a suitor comes. Unfortunately, she allowed the pressure of marriage to get to her and involved herself with various men who ended up abusing her physically and emotionally. It was so bad that she became emotionally unstable and insecure. She learnt the hard way. Life does not have to be that way.

There are so many people out there who, like this lady, are going through abusive relationships because they feel they are better off being in a violent relationship than not being in any relationship at all. It is a lie from the devil. Even Adam was single for a while before Eve was created.

Choosing to maximize your singleness positively is a wise decision that will pay off after marriage. Pursue your dreams; live your life to the fullest and at the right time, the right man or woman will come into your life. Do not halt your plans and future in the hope of pursuing them when you find a life partner. Singleness is a vital stage of life and no matter how long or short it lasts, make the most of it!

Dealing With Insecurity

It is so sad to know that tens of millions of people around the world are plagued with this condition called "insecurity". The funny thing however, is that some people do not even know they suffer from it.

People feel insecure for various reasons. Personally, I feel so sad when I see single people who feel insecure around married people just because they are not yet married.

Another awful thing with insecurity is that it does not just affect the people who display it; it also affects the relationships they have with the people around them. Insecure single people do not make life difficult for themselves alone; they also make life difficult for people who relate with them. Many relationships and marriages are broken down today because one or both parties were insecure.

Insecurity makes you suspicious unnecessarily. It makes you suspect your friends, spouse or spouse-to-be even if they are not up to anything devious.

The best time to deal with insecurity is while you are still single. Be happy with who and how you are. Improve on the areas of your life that need improvement without envying people around you. Do not feel less or more important than the people around you as this is unhealthy for you and your relationships.

There are different forms of insecurity, but they reveal themselves in two different ways:

a) Timid insecurity

and

b) Self-important insecurity.

Timid Insecurity: This is the form of insecurity that makes people feel low about their life. They feel everyone around them is better than they are. This could be the result of circumstances surrounding their childhood or an event that left the feeling of low self-esteem in their mind. They sometimes act shy, inhibited, withdrawn or reserved.

People in this category always take people's opinion about them seriously. Comments made about their appearance, attitude and general conduct are very important to them, and they can make them feel happy or devastated.

We are all unique and we are all important. If you fall into this category, it is vital you believe in yourself. Feeling timid robs you of a fulfilled life. Life is short and to make the most of it is to live freely. Believe in whom God has made you, discover and celebrate your strengths so you can be a blessing to others. You are made in the very image of God.

It is important to note that there is a huge difference between TIMIDITY and HUMILITY. You can be humble without being timid, and timidity is not necessarily a sign of humility. Do not mistake one for the other.

Being timid hinders you from expressing yourself to the fullest. It steals opportunities from you and prevents you from maximizing your moments. You have something unique to offer your world; do not allow timidity to rob you of this wonderful experience.

Self-Important Insecurity: This is a form of insecurity that is mostly offensive in nature. People who fall under this category are very good at putting other people down just to feel good about themselves. They always want to be seen as important. They are scared of anyone around them who seems to be stealing the limelight from them.

Leaders who have this trait tend to suppress any thriving subordinate under them; they see them as threats. They constantly watch their backs so that their deputies, colleagues or subordinates do not outshine them. They hardly see anything good in other people. They can be very controlling and manipulative; they will not stop until they achieve their aim. They can get so engrossed with what they do to remain on top or get attention. They feed on recognition and respect. They do not welcome anything that puts them down. They are under the constant psychological fear that someone might out-do them.

The best way to handle such people is to be honest with them. They may not like you for it, but you will be offering them a lifeline that might help them in the long run. However, if you fall under this category, it is important you know that in life, there will always be people who are more than you in various aspects, and your ability to work with them without feeling insecure is an asset that will make a huge difference for you positively.

Feeling too important is not the same as being confident. Insecurity has deluded a lot of people and corrupted a lot of motives. That is why it is possible to carry out a good act with a bad motive.

Insecurity has broken homes, friendships and many other relationships, because it leads to suspicion – and suspicion is extremely dangerous.

Be yourself, respect others and rid yourself of any trace of insecurity in order to be the best you can be. Life is sweeter when we live it to the fullest and when it is void of insecurity. Being single does not make you less human or better than other people.

The Benefits of Singleness

Life is in phases and only wise people recognize and enjoy the various phases life offers us. It is always amusing when I see kids who are in a hurry to become adults and adults who are trying so hard to reverse the ageing process and stay young. Kids who are in a hurry to grow up fail to grasp the fact that they will grow up one day and adults who are trying hard to look young fail to embrace the truth that they cannot stop ageing. Plastic surgery, exercise, and a "wonder diet" may give you a youthful look on the surface, but inside you, the ageing process continues.

There is nothing wrong in doing things to maintain good health or look fit, but not at the expense of enjoying whatever season of life that you are in. If you are young, enjoy your youthful days and spend them wisely; if you are getting older, do not be scared of ageing. It is natural to grow old, so enjoy your old age. I often say, "Life is a free gift from God, but only a few get to enjoy it."

On the other hand, some parents put pressure on their children to grow up too quickly by pushing them into hobbies, contests, careers, events, training, etc. at the very expense of their childhood. Some of these kids grow up and later become depressed or suicidal because they were robbed of their childhood by their parents. Sometimes the motives of these parents are selfish.

There is nothing wrong with making a child understand and respect life's values or encouraging them to have the drive to achieve great things in life, but it is expedient that we also give them the opportunity to be kids and enjoy that special phase of their lives.

The phase of singleness should not be seen as boring, as some see it. Many single people spend a lot of their single days worrying about when to marry, who to marry, how to marry or if they will ever get married. They do this at the expense of enjoying their single life. The irony is that while many single people are in a hurry to marry, some married people wish they'd made the most of their single days, and some even desire to be single again. There are many benefits attached to singleness and the earlier you discover and explore them the better.

Some of the benefits of singleness are as follows:

~ *Purpose Discovery*:

More important than discovering your life partner is the need to discover your purpose in life. And the best time to discover your purpose is while you are still single.

It is very crucial for every one to discover and maximize his or her purpose in life. Everyone has a God-given purpose, but some people never get to discover theirs. Some people discover their purposes early in life and some people discover it late in life. It is better to discover your purpose late in life than not discovering it at all. However, it is even much better to discover your purpose early in life as a single person, as this will help you invest more time in exploring your purpose before meeting your spouse. When your spouse-to-be meets you fulfilling your purpose, it will be easier for him or her to partner with you along the way.

Many people discover their purposes in life long after they get married, and in some cases, it can take a toll on the entire family due to inconvenient adjustments that may have to be made. For instance, a married person with kids, who has been a teacher all his life, will have some major things to sort out if he suddenly decides that his purpose is to contribute to world peace by becoming a soldier. Pursuing this intention will take a toll on the family because his wife and kids would have to learn to get used to the lifestyle of soldiers, which may involve going to war, being away from home for long periods of time etc.

These adjustments may have a negative effect on the wife and children if it is not handled properly. However, if he had discovered this purpose earlier as a single person, his spouse would have known ahead of time the kind of future that was ahead of him and prepared for it.

This does not mean that married people cannot cope with the changes that come as a result of one or both spouses discovering their purposes in life or other changes that may transpire in life; it is just a lot easier and better to discover your purpose in life as a single person so that people around you will know what you are about.

A defined life is a life that is so clear in terms of purpose, and anyone that comes close, knows what such a life is all about. What is your purpose in life? As a single person, this question should continually be on your mind until you find the right answer; and when you do, explore it to the fullest.

~ *Undivided Attention:*

Another benefit of singleness is undivided attention. As a single person, you can afford to invest more of your time and energy in what you love doing most. It is not enough to discover your purpose; you have to invest time into it, and being single gives you the opportunity of doing that.

41

Married people naturally take their spouses into consideration in all they do, and if children are involved, they come into the equation too. An unmarried person does not have a wife or children to worry about. Such a person can focus more on whatever he or she wants to do or achieve in life.

Apostle Paul tells us in 1 Corinthians 7:32-35 that the unmarried person has more time and less distraction for "things of the Lord" more than the person who is married. The "things of the Lord" is not just referring to going to church; it also includes doing and being what God has designed you to be and accomplishing what He wanted you to do in life.

Marriage does not hinder progress at all. In fact, marrying the right person can enhance your purpose and life. That is why the Bible says in **Proverbs 18:22: "Whoever finds a wife, finds a good thing and obtains FAVOUR from the Lord."**

There are many married people out there who, regardless of their commitment to family, still succeed at their passion and purpose much more than some single people. I strongly believe that when we commit our ways unto the Lord and give our best, He will cause us to excel regardless of the challenges that may come our way.

~ *Maximum Flexibility:*

Single people can enjoy flexibility to maximum levels. When you are married, you need to make major decisions jointly with your spouse. However, as a single person you can make your decisions while you are on the move. You can relocate geographically to wherever you want, buy whatever you want, invest in any venture you like, work late hours as often as you want to, etc. You are flexible with a lot of things.

Your flexibility is responsibly tailored when you are married, because you have to consider the person or people in your life. A brother of mine used to be a chronic workaholic when he was single. As a music producer, he worked odd hours sequencing, voicing and mixing songs; he travelled for concerts, went on tours and to various events as often as he could. But, when he got married to the love of his life, he began turning some offers down in order to spend time with his family; and his flexibility was adjusted by his new responsibility of being a husband. He is one of the few people I know who has made the most of their flexibility when they were single. Make the most of your flexibility while it lasts!

If you are married, not being as flexible as you were when you were single is not a bad thing; it is only a sign that you are in a different phase of life. Enjoy it because you can succeed at whatever you want in life whether you are married or not. Getting married to an understanding spouse will not hinder you from fulfilling your purpose. You may have to tailor your activities, but you do not have to abandon or halt your purpose!

~ Risks:

If you are person who loves taking risks, there is really no limit to the risks you can take as a single person. These risks could be in any area of your life.

I have seen many single people who took huge financial risks most people would consider crazy. A good number of such risks paid off. For those that did not really get their desired results, life still went on for them because they were solely responsible and answerable to themselves as far as that risk was concerned. A responsible married man or woman will usually need to consult with his or her spouse before taking any huge risk.

I remember a few years ago, a friend of mine who was single decided to take a huge risk by abandoning his promising career in the United Kingdom to go to a developing country to start a business. It was a move many thought was crazy but, since he was single and answerable only to himself, he went ahead to start his real estate business in an environment many felt was not safe or stable for investment. A few years later, his business became a massive success; much more than he anticipated.

Today, he is a source of inspiration to his friends. He took a risk that could have gone either way, but went ahead anyway because he was single. If he were married, he would have gone through various stages of consultation with his family before making such a move.

Although many married people do take risks and many do succeed at some of their ventures, it is a lot easier to take risks as a single person. A single person can decide to take a risk in any area of his or her life and embrace the consequences without much fear.

It is important, however, that you do not take a risk just because everyone is taking a risk; you should think wisely and do what your heart tells you to do.

Section 2

Chapter Four
Preparation

Preparation determines performance, and knowledge is power!

People find it natural to study before going for examinations; they find it natural to research before starting a business; they investigate the stock market before investing; they put in years of study and work to excel in a career, etc. Yet millions of people across the globe approach marriage with little or no preparation.

Humans are about the most complex organism in existence. Some people do not even understand themselves, yet they want to jump into a relationship and get to know someone else.

Succeeding in a relationship or marriage is not a function of age, intelligence, chance, wealth, religion or disposition. It is a function of adequate preparation, commitment, dedication, sacrifice and unconditional love. These qualities need to be learnt and developed over time.

The majority of people that get married today have little or no knowledge of what they are going into. Reading healthy relationship books, attending marriage conferences and seminars and courses are things I consider very crucial for anyone who intends to get married someday.

You need to equip yourself with the relevant knowledge in order to succeed in any endeavour you want to embark on.

The scriptures declare in Luke 14:28: "For which of you, intending to build a tower, does not sit down first and count the cost, whether he has enough to finish it?" What do you know about love, commitment, conflict resolution, faithfulness, sacrifice, etc? These things will stare you in the face someday when you go into a serious relationship.

Most single people spend nearly all of their time thinking about their wedding day. They fail to put as much time into preparing for the reality of marriage. The wedding is just an event that lasts for a few hours, but marriage is meant to be for life. It is not wise to invest more time and resources into the wedding than the main thing, which is life after the wedding.

All some single people do during courtship is jump from one fancy restaurant to another. They allow marriage to take them by surprise and eventually discover that they were not prepared for the journey.

Invest in your marital future by preparing yourself with necessary knowledge. Even though your knowledge will not prevent you from facing challenges, you will be better equipped to face them than someone who is not prepared at all.

Centuries ago, men and women were prepared for marriage from a very young age. Some were even betrothed from birth. Their parents taught them fundamental things they needed to know about the person they were betrothed to and about the marriage institution. No wonder marriages worked better then.

Most bachelors and spinsters in that era went into marriage having a good idea of what they were going into. Even as recently as the 1940s and 1950s, making marriage work was not the responsibility of the married couple alone; parents and the society at large played a role in making homes work. Societies had a conscience and their moral compass was still functional to a high degree.

If a marriage failed, it was not seen as the failure of the couple involved alone, but the failure of the two families involved. People were eager to make their relationships work – unlike today where many people are constantly looking for cheap excuses to abandon their relationships and marriages.

If you want to be in a relationship that would last a lifetime (just as people confess when taking their marriage vows), then we need to change our approach to relationships and marriage. Let us look at some things we need to know in order to be better equipped for a genuine relationship or marriage:

10 Truths About True Love:

We live in a world where many people are quick to use the word "love" without really meaning it or knowing its implication. It is, therefore, important to weigh the gravity and discern the sincerity attached to the word when you or someone else uses it.

"Love" is word we are meant to use consciously; it is a word that has a lot responsibilities attached to it. Sadly, the word "love" means nothing to so many people in this generation. People casually say they are in "love" with someone, when in reality what they want is a casual relationship, sex or an affair.

Another thing I consider so tragic is when I see people who have a good understanding of love getting entwined in a relationship with people who have no value for love. When this happens, struggles are inevitable.

Below are some core truths about real or true love:

1. Love Goes Beyond Feelings: Feelings come and go. They are energized and propelled mainly by circumstances, emotions and desires. If you choose to see love just as a feeling, then you have got it twisted. The truth of the matter is that lust is a feeling and infatuation is also a feeling.

Failure to differentiate between lust and infatuation and love has landed many people in relationships they never should have gone into in the first place. So many are heartbroken today because what they thought was going to last forever vanished into thin air in no time. Indeed, one or both parties in the relationship had misconceptions about true love. Do not mistake "feelings" for "love"; let feelings be a by-product of someone's true love for you or your true love for someone else.

King Henry VIII of England was a man who can testify to the fact that "feeling" is not the same thing as "love". King Henry lived in the 14th Century. He had six wives in his lifetime aside from the many suspected affairs he had outside his marriages.

His first wife, Catherine of Aragon, though a devout Christian, was not enough for him. While married to her, he started having feelings for another woman (Anne Boleyn), the woman he eventually divorced his wife for. The marriage was short-lived and Anne was later beheaded. I strongly believe that if it was true love, it wouldn't have ended that way.

If you operate in the realm of "feelings", your relationships will not last because, when you develop a stronger feeling for someone else, you will end up leaving the person you were in a relationship with.

After Anne Boleyn's execution, the king later married Jane Seymour, a lady he took interest in while he was still married to his second wife Anne. Jane tragically died shortly after giving birth to a son. About three years later, the King married his fourth wife, Anne of Cleves, and divorced her that same year (1540). In 1540 he married Kathryn Howard only to have her executed two years later. He finally married Katherine Parr who was his wife until he died about three years after their marriage.

True love makes you totally committed and dedicated to one relationship at a time. If you allow feelings alone to drive you, you will not be able to stay committed to a relationship.

King Henry VIII kept drifting from one woman to the other and though married, he could not stay faithful to any of his wives. Imagine the heartache, grief and frustrations those women went through.

A man or woman driven solely by feelings is a person that will find it so hard to stay faithful to one relationship at a time, and a person who will also give so many people grief in relationships.

2. Inner Peace: Regardless of your external challenges or the circumstances surrounding you, where true love exists, there is an inner peace that strengthens you from within. Philippians 4:7 says, "And the peace of God, which passes all understanding, shall keep your heart and minds through Christ."

This scripture is so true. I strongly recommend that before you go into a relationship, you need to have this inner peace. If you are about to go into a relationship and deep within you, you are not experiencing this peace, I strongly advise that you pause. You need to be comfortable with the person you will be in a relationship with; this comfort is best propelled by the inner peace you will experience. What is the point of being in a relationship with someone that your heart is not comfortable with? Even if everything looks fine on the outside but you do not feel comfortable inside you, then you have every reason to pause. On the other hand, sometimes, the circumstances around you may be chaotic and you might still have the inner peace that energizes you from within to carry on with the relationship. Though this inner peace is felt from within us, its source is God.

Most times, people jump into relationships without minding the signals they receive from within. Even if people around you do not feel good about the relationship, it is crucial that both parties to a relationship have this peace about relating with each other. There is no hindrance for parties to a relationship who experience this peace except that they give in to external pressures. This peace surpasses human understanding because it does not always make sense to parties outside it.

People may point to many reasons why you should abandon a relationship and wonder why you still want to go ahead, but they would not understand what you feel from within. When we allow God to go ahead of us in our relationships and marriages, we would make fewer mistakes and worry less.

I remember when I was courting my wife. Shortly before our wedding, some circumstances came up and ordinarily, a few people that knew about it thought we would bail. My wife and I prayed and we both had peace from within to go ahead. Some people could not understand why we were happy to go ahead.

We experienced inner peace in spite of the external challenges and went ahead. Whenever we look back now, we celebrate and thank God that we did not quit. The challenges began to melt as we took a step based on the convictions we both had. We are reaping the dividends of that peace today.

On the contrary, many have landed themselves in disastrous relationships because of the absence of this inner peace at the beginning of their relationship. A lady recently told me how she went ahead to marry a man she never had peace about. A few years down the line, she suffered severe abuse and neglect. Do not allow people to pressure you into a relationship or into anything you do not have peace about.

3. Honesty: In a relationship characterized by true love, honesty flows like a spring. True love makes people naturally open to each other without the fear of being taken for granted, because true love is void of deception.

I always wonder why these days so many people find it easy to lie to the people they claim to love. When you go into a serious relationship with someone, it is very important that you are open and honest. Keeping dark secrets from the person you love is one sure way of ruining the relationship.

Years ago, I had a chat with a group of single ladies, most of who were in relationships. Almost unanimously, they maintained that there are some things they would never tell the person they are in a relationship with. I was curious and asked why. In reply, they said that their previous experiences taught them not to be open and honest. They claimed that being honest about some personal issues might either scare guys away or make the guys love them for the wrong reasons. They were ready to go as far as concealing vital information like the number of children they had from previous relationships, how much they earned and the investments they had.

I tried to make them understand that true love has no secrets. Sadly, some married couples do the same; they keep secrets from each other. When you truly love and trust someone, you will be open with them. Love makes us vulnerable sometimes; being open is a risk that people in love take.

After much discussion with the ladies, I made them to see the need to let go of the negative residue from their previous relationships, and to treat people individually without branding everyone as the same. I always tell people, "All men are not the same and all women are not the same." Don't move around assuming all men or women are the same, we are not! There are still good men and women out there!

Today, two out of the four ladies are married. They decided to be honest about their lives, including the not-so-good bits they thought would work against them. Instead of working against them, it made their men to love them even more for being very honest.

The thing with being dishonest is that you cannot conceal the truth forever; it will always prevail. It might take years or even decades, but it always comes out. Many relationships and marriages have been destroyed today because one party to the relationship discovered vital information the other party concealed from them. It becomes more complicated when your spouse, fiancé or fiancée discovers a secret you have been hiding. This will kill trust quickly and break the heart of the person you are in a relationship with.

Be honest with the person you love. Wisely reveal the things you know are crucial and important to the future of the relationship, especially when you are at a serious stage. Do not wait until it is too late and do not be afraid he or she might leave you. If they truly love you and if it is meant to be, then nothing will discourage them from pursuing a relationship with you.

4. High Value: Placing a high value on the person you love without selfish expectations or pay back is one of the signs of true love in a relationship. This value is placed on who the person is rather than what the person has.

Honestly, the value you place on the person you claim to love can determine if you really love them or not. So many people have little or no regard for the person they claim to love. In a relationship or marriage where people do not place a value on their spouses, abuse becomes the order of the day. If you place value on a thing, you will not abuse it; instead, you will protect it.

Some people place a higher value on their cars, jewellery or other material possessions than they do on their loved ones. In today's world, it is pretty normal to insure our houses, cars, jewellery, etc. because we place value on them.

Some people have security cameras and other sophisticated gadgets to keep their homes safe. Yet, the people they claim to love are left unattended, unprotected and uncared for. What is love if it is void of care and protection?

Are you in a relationship with a person and do not care about their wellbeing? Chances are you do not really love them. If you do, these things will come to you naturally. If you value the person you are in a relationship with, you will not trample on them; you will listen to them; you will consult them before making a crucial decision that involves them; you will cherish them and respect them.

When you value the person you love, you are indirectly placing value on yourself as well. Treat the person you love like a queen or a king and they will in turn treat you like royalty!

5. Being Yourself: Most relationships these days are what I call "programmed relationships". I call them "programmed" because instead of freely living their lives, many people in relationships consciously program themselves to act, talk and look a certain way just to please the person they are in a relationship with. People pretend to be something else to please someone or get someone's approval.

If you have to pretend to please the person you claim to love, then the question for you is: how long can you keep up the act? You can only pretend for a time; afterwards, you will get tired and just want to be yourself.

When you eventually decide to be yourself, the person you were trying to please all along will become even more displeased because they will feel deceived and mislead by you. They may even go as far as calling you a hypocrite, which is not too far from the truth. Please, be yourself!

True love makes you free enough to be yourself. Stop living someone else's life; live your life freely and someone will love you for who you really are. Do not pretend in a relationship; feel free to be yourself because trying to be someone else will only make you end up as a duplicate. Be original. Be yourself.

NOTE: Do not waste your precious life and time on a relationship that is heading nowhere.

6. It is Patient: "Love is patient and kind; it is not jealous or conceited or proud; love is not ill-mannered or selfish or irritable; love does not keep records of wrong" (1 Corinthians 13:4).

The above scripture paints a true picture of what love really is. Sadly, what many people now call love is far from the reality of this scripture.

The first word the Bible used in defining love in this scripture is "patience". It is an essential characteristic of love that you must understand if you want to be in a long-lasting relationship.

In today's world, where almost everything is fast-paced, it might be difficult to remember this virtue called "patience". With patience, understanding and communication become a lot easier for parties in a relationship.

Lack of patience has made many people miss out on God's original plan for them in their relationships, and as a result, they settled for less than what God intended for them. Many homes are broken today because some parties were not patient enough to work things out. Many parties to a relationship no longer want to fix their problems. They are so in a hurry to replace each other with someone else. They think that by doing so, their problems will be solved.

I remember decades ago when husbands and wives stood by each other firmly in the days of trouble. They held hands and told each other "we will get through this." They had faith and were committed to each other; they were willing to stick to the vows they made on the altar against all odds. These days, people no longer mean what they say, even at the altar of God. If we promised "for better for worse" at the altar, then it should be for better for worse in reality.

Would you throw your 2012 Continental GT Bentley away just because it got a dent or just because the rear view mirror was broken? Of course not! You would get it fixed. Your spouse is worth much more than a Bentley! Do not be in a hurry to abandon your relationship because of a challenge; instead, patiently work things through. You will be glad you did.

Sometimes, trouble may come to break you, but if you patiently hold on tight, it will only make you and your relationship stronger.

7. Sexual Purity: Where true love exists, parties would keep their relationship pure until the right time (marriage). Although it's seen by some as a primitive practice, Romans 12:2 says, "Be not conformed to this world, but be ye transformed by the renewing of your mind." We should not do things just because everyone is doing it.

Your body is the temple of the Holy Spirit and we shall account for it someday before God. As a single person, having sexual intercourse with someone you are not married to is very dangerous. Apart from the risk of being infected with sexually transmitted diseases, there is a spiritual undertone to it as well. The things that happen in the physical realm are just a reflection of the realities in the spirit realm. There is a spiritual side to every sexual activity.

During sexual intercourse between unmarried people, there is also a transfer of spirits between parties involved. So many people have exposed themselves to demonic manipulation and oppression because they had sex with someone who is demon possessed or someone who is oppressed by the powers of darkness. In contrast, sex between married couples is an honourable act. It is very important to remember always that our body is the temple of the Holy Spirit, and we ought to keep it clean.

8. It Protects: In Genesis 2:25, the Bible says, "And they were both naked, the man and his wife and they were not ashamed." Apart from the basic meaning of this scripture, it also means that they protected each other. Their nakedness (limitation, challenges and weaknesses) was open to both of them, but they were not ashamed because they protected each other.

Do not celebrate your friend's weaknesses or expose them to other people just to ridicule them. You are in their lives for a reason, so do not use what they tell you in trust against them on a later date.

It is your responsibility to protect the person you love. Do not join others to destroy or castigate them. We live in a very selfish world now where people are eager to protect their interests first before that of anyone else. This should not be the case! As a hen protects her chicks from danger, so should we also protect the people we love – not just in words, but also in action.

9. It Forgives: Sometimes, the people we love the most hurt us the most. In the light of this fact, there is no love without forgiveness. We are imperfect beings heading towards perfection and are prone to do or say something that may offend our friends.

Are you in a relationship with someone you love? If yes, that person may have offended you in times past and if they haven't, they will in the future. Most of the things we do or say that offend our loved ones are not usually intentional; even if they are, where the power of forgiveness exists, the offence can be overcome.

Forgiveness is key to our daily living, so much so that Jesus, in His response to Peter's question on how many times we should forgive our brothers or sisters in a day, said we should forgive 70 x 7 times (Mathew 18:21-22). This is a total of 490 times in a single day. If forgiveness wasn't that important, Jesus would not have said so.

The champion of forgiveness, Jesus Christ, demonstrated to us on the highest level what forgiveness really is; He was crucified by the very people He came to save, yet He was able to say, "Father forgive them."

True love is always sustained by forgiveness. Unforgiveness between couples will hinder their prayers and spiritual growth. It can also prevent them from receiving forgiveness as well. "For if you forgive men their trespasses, your Heavenly father will also forgive you" (Matthew 6:14).

Unforgiveness leads to anger, malice, strife and every work of darkness; where these evil things abound, the devil reigns supreme. On your own, you may find it very hard to forgive some offences, but with the help of the Holy Spirit, you will experience the extraordinary grace and power to forgive.

I was touched when a lady shared with me years ago how she forgave her husband who cheated on her a few months after they got married. She received a very powerful revelation on forgiveness and forgave her husband that she loved so much. Her husband was in so much shock that she could forgive him. He assumed that she was going to end the relationship as a result of his actions, but the power of forgiveness stepped in.

Another dangerous thing about unforgiveness is that it hinders the person that carries the unforgiving heart more than anyone else. The feeling of pain and disappointment can develop into depression. It is better to let go and allow God to heal your heart and mind through His love as you forgive the people that offend you. A relationship void of forgiveness is a relationship that has a bleak future.

10. It Never Dies: "Many waters cannot quench love or drown it" (Songs of Solomon 8:7). True love thrives against all odds. The rate at which people fall in and out of love is alarming in our generation. You may see a couple holding hands and professing their undying love for each other today, and then before you know it, the same couple are committing their love to totally different people.

True love is a force that is stronger than a tornado or a tsunami; even in the face of opposition, it can still thrive if parties in it are persistent. The above scripture tells us that many waters cannot quench love. In other words, regardless of the trouble and challenges of life, love can still prevail. Many couples are quick to quit their relationships or marriages just because of a test or trial. I have seen so many relationships end because a party to the relationship lost their job, had a health issue, etc. It is better you wait until you are very sure and understand what love is, before you profess love to anyone.

One major reason why the love that many profess fades away in relationships is because, these days, many people's love for each other is "conditional". True, sacrificial and selfless love is fading fast.

Most people now go into a relationship mainly for what they can get, which makes them focus mainly on what they can gain and not on the people they claim to love.

True love is worth fighting for, so do not give up on love easily. Do all you can to stand by the person you love through good and hard times.

Chapter Five

Seven Cardinal Pillars of Love Neglected by This Generation

On a daily basis I encounter people who say they are in love. They believe they are in love for various reasons. One question I like asking singles not yet in a relationship and desiring to fall in love someday is: "What is Love?"

The response I get from people varies from person to person. I noticed, however, that many people's perception of love was influenced by their culture, religion, experience and expectations.

Some people think love is all about kissing, romance, gifts, roses, sex, money, going out on a date, etc. The truth of the matter is that there is more to "love" than all of these things. Too many marriages, relationships and hearts are broken today because of people's misconceptions about this crucial word "love".

In my book "True Fulfillment", I wrote extensively on what love really is. In order for us to build viable, long-lasting relationships and marriages that stand the test of time, we need to know, understand, embrace and practice the following pillars of love. Without them, a relationship is bound to crumble.

Pillars of Love:

1. The Pillar of Sacrifice:- Genuine love involves sacrifice. In the course of a loving relationship, parties to it willingly sacrifice for each other. They go the extra mile for the person they love even if is causes them discomfort. It is very important that the willingness to sacrifice is mutual in a relationship because, if the sacrifice is one-sided, over time the party that always makes the sacrifice may get weary and the relationship may end up falling apart. Are you willing to lay down your life to protect or save the person you love? The scripture says in John 15:13 that, "Greater love hath no man than this, that a man lay down his life for his friends."

Our perfect example of love, Jesus Christ, laid down His life as a sign of His sacrificial love for us. My question for you today is: "How far are you willing to go for the one you love?"

I heard a story of a married couple years ago that made me laugh. They were fast asleep in their bedroom when their house was being burgled by armed men. The husband woke up first after hearing the sound of their door being forced open. He woke his wife and they realized they were about to be robbed. Surprisingly, the husband told his wife to go and see who was by the door while he remained in the bedroom peeping through the keyhole. Eventually, the burglars left when they heard movements within the house.

I find this story funny because the husband was not willing to put his life on the line to protect his wife, but his wife was. You cannot rule out sacrificing for the person you love in the course of your relationship.

Sacrificial acts come in various ways. I have seen circumstances where parties to relationships had to sacrifice by way of giving up their career to look after a sick spouse, move country or home for the sake of a spouse, give up a job to look after the children, etc. Many people give up on their relationships because they are faced with a situation that demands them to sacrifice for someone they claim they love.

This generation is quickly trying to erase sacrifice from their dictionary of love without realizing that for love to stand the test of time, it has to include sacrifice from both parties involved.

2. The Pillar of Giving:- Love is not complete without giving. When you are in love with someone, you give to him or her to show your love for them. The opening statement in John 3:16 says it all: "For God so loved the world that He GAVE his only begotten Son…" In that scripture, we see how God demonstrated His love for us by giving His only Son to us. When we are truly in love, we will gladly give time, attention, gifts, etc. to the people we love. The act of giving should be practiced by people in a loving relationship because giving goes a long way to making both parties feel valued and appreciated.

The person you are in a relationship with is like a garden; and what you sow in them is what you will eventually reap. Having this understanding will enable you to practice giving with so much joy because in reality, when you give to the person you love, you are indirectly giving to yourself. True love cannot be separated from giving because they go hand in hand.

It is very important that whatever you give should not be out of duress. Give freely from your heart. Don't just be the receiving type in a relationship; strive to give what you can, your time, money, energy, etc. For the scripture says, it is more blessed to give than to receive (Acts 20:35).

3. The Pillar of Correction and Rebuke:- If you claim to be in love with someone and you cannot correct them when they are going astray, then something is wrong. Would you allow the person you love dearly to fall into a dangerous ditch just because you do not want to offend them? Falling into a ditch is more serious than being offended. This generation has removed this vital pillar of love away from their relationships, and as a result, we are seeing people who

cannot tell right from wrong because of a major deficiency in their moral compass. Failure to correct the person you love when they make mistakes or when they go astray, will make them keep making the same mistakes over and over again.

Many parents have ruined the lives of their children because they failed to rebuke and correct them when they were younger. As a result, some of them have ended up in jail or a crack house. Do not hold back rebuke and correction from the person you love when the situation calls for it. Open rebuke is better than secret love says the word (Proverbs 27:5). However, when we are correcting our loved one, let us do it in love.

4. The Pillar of Longevity:- Today's media constantly portrays love as something that is temporal and trivial. Love is a powerful force that is designed to stand the test of time and designed to last for a very long time; it is a long-term commitment and not a short-term arrangement. Many people fall in and out of love as often as they go to a grocery store and that makes me really wonder if they know what love truly means.

People walk up to the altar and make vows to love each other forever, but months down the line they are thinking of going their separate ways. God has loved us with an everlasting love, so much so that He is willing to forgive us our sins anytime we ask Him to. This is the sign of His undying love for us. Are you in a relationship? Make a commitment to make it last against all odds.

5. The Pillar of Forgiveness:- Love and forgiveness, as we covered earlier, always go hand in hand. There is no true love without forgiveness. While we were yet sinners, Christ died for us in order to forgive us our sins. Forgiveness is vital to any relationship that will go the distance.

6.   The Pillar of Patience:- We also touched on patience earlier, a vital pillar that holds people in love together. This is an indispensable pillar indeed.

7.   The Pillar Called "God":- God is love. A relationship void of the presence of God is a relationship that is indirectly void of love. If you take God out of your relationship, your relationship will become susceptible to all manners of pressure, and it may eventually fall apart.

Psalm 11:3: "If the foundation be destroyed, what shall the righteous do?" Wise people involve God in their relationships from the very beginning and if God builds your relationship, you are guaranteed to have a very good union.

The picture of love can never be successfully painted without God in it. Do you want to build a strong, reliable and joyous relationship? If your answer is "yes", then make Jehovah the main pillar of your love life today!

Chapter Six

How To Discern The Right Life Partner

Millions of singles across the globe are on the lookout daily for someone they can call their life partner; a person they hope to go through life's journey with; someone they hope to call a husband or a wife; someone they desire to spend the rest of their lives with. There is a question I would like to ask every single person looking for a life partner. The question is: "Are you looking for a part-time or a full-time life partner?"

One of the bad things that can happen to people in a relationship is for one party to have a full-time mentality and the other to have a part-time mentality. This will make their commitment to and expectations for the relationship to be uneven, and, consequently create chaos.

Many singles make good decisions in their careers, businesses, finances, etc., but they get it all wrong when it comes to making the right choices in their relationships. It is crucial to understand the fact that even if you have everything going well for you, but fail to make the right choice in your relationship, it can affect your entire life and ruin areas that are presently going smoothly. I have seen many people who had everything going well for them until they made a marital decision that jeopardized their lives.

When and where you get married is not as important as who you marry. Regardless of your education, position, wealth and spirituality, if you marry the wrong person, struggle, bitterness and pain are inevitable.

A lady shared her sad story with me sometime back. She was raised in a Christian home and both of her parents were ministers of the gospel. It came to the time for her to get married and she decided to marry a guy who professed his love for her. Her spirit did not release her to go ahead, and the voice of the Spirit did not approve of the relationship. She decided to go ahead anyway and what followed afterwards was pathetic. She went through a lot of horrible experiences; she was oppressed, tormented, suppressed and depressed by the powers of darkness for many years in her marriage before she eventually encountered the power of God and got delivered. Those years of pain and oppression would have been averted if only she discerned and hearkened to the voice of the Holy Spirit.

I met another lady recently who had endured an abusive relationship. She had decided to go into the relationship for all the wrong reasons, and almost lost her mind in the process. God came to her rescue and today she is enjoying the liberating power of God. If she had known how to choose better, those years of pain would have been avoided.

Why would you want to do life with the wrong person? It is far better to marry late and have a low budget wedding than to rush into a marriage, have a 5-star wedding and end up with the wrong person. Getting married to the wrong person will only lead to a life of misery.

The problem for so many singles today is that they cannot differentiate between the right and the wrong person. The Bible made us understand in Genesis 2:20 that although Adam was surrounded by all manner of plants and animals, there was no helper suitable for him until Eve came. The same should apply in our day; you may be surrounded by all kinds of people, but it takes discernment to know which one is suitable for you as a man; and it also takes discernment to know which marriage proposal to accept as a single lady.

Marriage is not just about the diamond ring, honeymoon and expensive wedding gown; it is the life after the wedding that really counts. If your happiness is paramount to you, then you will not leave the decision of the person you choose to marry in the hands of chance, you will discern it by the help of the Holy Spirit.

Discernment is the ability to judge well; being able to grasp and comprehend what is obscure. It is being able to see beyond the naked eye, beyond the visible. As believers, our discernment is powered by the Spirit of God who knows everything. Many important details of people's lives cannot be seen with the naked eye. In other words, someone may look great on the outside and tick all the boxes for a good husband or wife, but when you activate your discernment, you may see things about the person that are concealed. It pays to use your discernment when choosing a life-partner.

Many men and women have ended up in the wrong relationships, marriages and homes because of a lack of discernment. Do not be easily carried away by the external features of people; instead, inquire of the Lord and He will reveal the hidden things about them to you.

Why We Need Discernment:

A~ *To avoid deception*: Many people claim to be what they are not; they put on a false identity and appear harmless. Many singles like to impress the people they hope to be in a relationship with. They go to great lengths to masquerade themselves and give misleading impressions contrary to who they really are on the inside.

Discernment, therefore, is a vital tool that will deliver you from being deceived by pretenders. Why get into a relationship or marriage only to be surprised later by the discovery that the person you tied the knot with is not who he or she appeared to be at the beginning? I have encountered so many men and women who were victims of deception in relationships.

Years ago, a lady who was so dedicated to the Lord in her local church met a man who seemed to meet all the requirements she wanted in her dream man. He appeared very pious and his lips were full of religious lingo. He was always eager to arrange prayer meetings and fasted regularly. The lady was swept off her feet with the attributes this man seemed to posses. They dated for a while and he later proposed marriage to her. Eventually, they got married.

A few months into their marriage, she started to notice a decline in his spiritual activities and commitments. She overlooked it and carried on hoping things would change for the better. Unfortunately, things got worse. He went out of control and became unfaithful, abusive and very negligent towards his duties as a husband. She became so frustrated that her health was affected. She later discovered the bitter truth; that he moved into the city where she was with one mission in mind, which was to find a good Christian church girl to marry. He was never spiritual or committed to the things of God in the first place; he had to put on an act in order to deceive someone into marriage.

In the previous city where he lived, he was known as someone who was unstable, unfaithful and full of lies. When I asked the lady if she prayed about the relationship before she got into it, she was very honest in her response; she said that she did not bother to pray because he appeared spiritual and was committed to the things of God; that the majority of her friends thought he was a Godsend. Too many people are victims of this kind of deception.

It is very important to operate in discernment when you are about to make an important decision like proposing marriage or accepting a marriage proposal. Irrespective of how someone looks and appears on the outside, it is needful to scan them through the lens of discernment.

A guy told me years ago how he married a lady because he thought she was rich. She gave him an impression that she was very wealthy. She bought him expensive gifts while they were dating, paid his bills and even offered to pay for their wedding. While they were dating, she would always talk about a business deal she is working on, her real estate business in a different city, etc.

A few months after they got married, however, she could not pretend anymore. It became clear that she was in debt and there were no real estate, investment or business deals anywhere. He felt betrayed and cheated because of this deception, which was made easier by his greed. If he wasn't greedy and if he operated in discernment, things would have been different for him.

Don't just fall for someone because of their outward appearance or what they say they are. Look beyond what the naked eyes can see. Ask the Lord to reveal their real identity to you. There are so many wolves in sheep's clothing today that have mastered the acts and ways of the sheep; and if you do not operate in discernment, you will fall victim to their schemes.

There is no point lying to someone about your age, financial status or marital status in order to get them into a relationship with you. Be yourself and be real. The place of discernment prior to going into a relationship or marriage should not be taken for granted. Operate in discernment and the obscure details will be revealed to you.

B~ *To see hidden potential:* On a positive note, operating in discernment makes you see the hidden potential embedded in someone. We meet people who are at various stages in their lives; not every suitor will come as a finished product. Without adequate discernment, a man or woman can lose out on a potentially great relationship.

We are all gifted naturally with abilities and talents that can potentially make us successful. However, it is one thing to have potential, and another thing for the potential to be explored.

There are different ways to spot and explore someone's potential. Some people's potential is spotted and explored by the help of the people around them, while some people discover and explore their potential in life themselves. When it comes to choosing a life partner, we have to be careful not to assess people based on their visible abilities and strengths alone. If we look deep enough, we may see that they have potential to be great tomorrow.

I have seen many relationships that started with little or no external trace of success, but over time, both parties became very successful in life because they saw promising potential in each other, and believed in each other until these potentials were fully explored.

Some years ago, a lady I knew very well accepted a marriage proposal from a man her family considered to be a failure. He had an unsecure job that paid little and, even though he always appeared tidy, the quality of his clothing was nothing to write home about. In the midst of the opposition, one thing was firm and that was her love for this young man. Most of her family members advised her to forget about him and wait for someone with a brighter future, but she refused.

Eventually, with weak support from her parents and some of her siblings, she got married to him. She told her friends and family that she saw a bright future ahead of them and that there was something unique about the guy. And she was right!

A year after they got married, not only did his job become permanent, he also got a double promotion. All along the guy had exceptional managerial skills embedded inside of him, but not everyone around him recognised it.

With her help, he worked on his natural managerial skills and his boss took note of him when he came up with some lovely ideas that revolutionized the company. In less than three years into their marriage, they were living the dream life.

He was given a special position in the company where he worked; he was no longer just an employee but a partner. They were so blessed to the point that the very people who despised her husband later came to them for help. The same man that was considered a low-life was later called a successful man. If his wife did not discern his true potential, she may have missed out on the great relationship they have today.

Many men and women have missed out on potentially great relationships because they could not discern what the future held for the people they encountered. Many singles are just interested in meeting Mister or Miss "Perfect"; they do not want to be part of the making of the success story. They forget that success is a lot sweeter when you are part of its making.

It is very important not to focus on someone's potential alone. There has to also be the will and passion to succeed by the man or woman who has the potential. Without passion and action, inherent potential will remain dormant.

C~ *In the midst of confusion:* One of the times many people get confused the most is when they are about to choose a life partner or say "yes" to a marriage proposal. It can be a chaotic situation, especially if family and friends have conflicting opinions about your intended choice.

Our families and friends, in their bid to show how much they love and care for us, can sometimes become overbearing. If you have friends and family members with a strong opinion, you can get confused in the crucial moment of choosing a life partner. In the midst of the chaos and confusion caused by too many voices and choices, you can close your ears and eyes to what the people around you are saying, and discern for yourself which way to follow.

Many people have made the huge mistake of marrying the wrong man or woman because they made their decision under the pressure and influence of other people. The problem with marrying someone that your parents or friends pressure you to marry is that they will not live with you in the marriage.

Family and friends will come to your wedding to celebrate with you, but they will not live with you afterwards. It is, therefore, not wise to marry someone just to please your friends or loved ones. You need to be in love with the person you intend to marry.

Although we live in an era where it seems like there is a scarcity of responsible men and women ready for marriage, there are so many men and especially women out there who are constantly being bombarded by marriage proposals that they get so confused trying to decide who to say yes to. Seclude yourself from the noise emanating from your external environment and discern wisely.

Sometimes, the chaos and confusion may not come from your external environment alone, but from within you. When the voice of lust, greed, emotion and desire are speaking to your mind at the same time, it may be difficult to hear what the Spirit is saying.

Even in the midst of confusion, God still speaks. The question is, are we ready to listen, and can we differentiate the voice of the Holy Spirit from the voice of our emotions?

D~ *To successfully fulfil purpose:* The person you marry can determine if you fulfil your purpose in life successfully or not. I have seen so many vibrant men and women who started so well in life but were cut short in an untimely way as a result of the wrong marital choice. Your husband or wife is meant to be a suitable helper on this crucial journey of life. If you marry the wrong person, instead of receiving help, you will be distracted and will experience unprecedented setbacks.

Your purpose in life is as important as your life. Life to a certain degree is useless without a purpose of existence. So many people have thrown their purpose and calling away because of the person they ended up marrying. If you get married to someone who does not believe in your purpose, passion or calling, your life can end up being miserable.

At the beginning of many relationships, parties are lenient towards each other and may even pretend to be in support of whatever their future spouse is doing. But, months and years into the marriage, some spouses become a hindrance to the purpose and passion of their husbands or wives. Many people end up sacrificing their purpose in order to maintain peace in the home. This disaster can be avoided when we operate in discernment and choose the right helper on life's journey.

It is my earnest prayer that the Lord will help you to meet your suitable helper who will help you fulfil your purpose even as you also help them in fulfilling theirs.

E~ *Deliverance from disaster:* One of the best ways to avoid future disaster in marriage and in life as a whole is to operate in discernment. You can preserve and elongate your life when you hearken to the voice of discernment.

So many people are trapped in troubles and issues they could have avoided if they had operated in discernment earlier. It is one thing to see things the way they really are, and another thing to act in a decisive way that corresponds with what you have discerned.

Anytime we operate in discernment, a disaster waiting to happen in the future is averted; and anytime we fail to discern or act in line with what we have discerned, we fast-track our way into disaster. The benefit of operating in discernment cannot be quantified, as it delivers you from both seen and unseen danger. May the Lord deliver you from every disaster looming in your future as you wisely discern.

How NOT to Choose a Life Partner

Due to the many influences we have in our lives, our judgment can be affected negatively when it comes to choosing a life partner. Our cultures, the media, our environment, mentors, parents and friends influence our lives in a very powerful way. They shape our thinking and influence the decision-making process consciously and unconsciously. As a result, many choose their spouses the wrong way.

Below are some of the ways not to choose your spouse:

★ **In the flesh:** As good as your five senses are, it is not wise to make life-shaping decisions based on them alone. Our flesh is constantly at war with the Spirit. The flesh is naturally selfish and ceaselessly looks for ways to gratify itself. If you allow your eyes, ears, feelings, taste and sense of smell to dictate to you in life, you are bound to make expensive mistakes. There is nothing wrong with using your five senses to aid your choices, but to depend on them alone to shape your life is not wise. Our five senses have limitations; they can weigh physical things, but their judgment cannot go beyond the visible, material realms.

I recently met a man who told me that he is a victim of beauty. Quite amused, I wanted to know what he meant. He said his marriage was falling apart and he was sick and tired of the many challenges he was going through. I tried to make him understand that every marriage goes through challenges and that his was no exception. He then confessed that he never loved his wife from the beginning.

"Why did you marry her then?" I asked.

"I married her for the wrong reason; I married her only because of her beauty," he said, looking quite dejected.

He became captivated by her beauty the very first time he saw her. People always took note of her astonishing beauty anytime they attended social events together. The complements she got made him feel like a star, and he decided to marry her just for this reason. According to him, they had nothing in common and her character stank from the very start. However, he ignored all that and married her just because of the respect and compliments her beauty commanded for him from his friends. Years into the marriage and after several kids, the relationship broke down intolerably.

If you marry somebody because of their external qualities alone, you are likely to run into problems in the future. Although it is very important to be physically attracted to the person you intend to marry, that should not be the only reason. Someone's financial status, sexual orientation or nationality is not strong enough to hold a home together. Love needs to exist between both parties in the relationship. Where true love exists, every other external quality would be an added bonus.

In the book of Genesis chapter 27:1-46, the scripture gives us the account of how Isaac was deceived by Jacob and

Rebekah into diverting the blessings meant for Esau to Jacob. Although there was a word from the Lord to Rebekah when she was pregnant with twins that the elder (Esau) shall serve the younger (Jacob), it was not meant to happen in a fraudulent way.

Jacob connived with his mother and pretended to be Esau by putting on goatskin because Esau was a hairy man. Isaac was in doubt when Jacob came before him and pretended to be Esau. He could tell that the voice did not sound like that of his son Esau, yet he decided to dissolve his doubt by asking Jacob to come closer so he could FEEL him. When Isaac felt Jacob, his hands touched the goat's skin and he was deceived into thinking that Jacob was Esau. In life, when we make crucial decisions based on our feelings alone, we can be led astray.

One of the things that stimulates our flesh is our feelings. Unfortunately, feelings are not always reliable; they are temporal because they come and go. Your flesh cannot see far into the future. If, therefore, you choose a life partner based on the dictates of your flesh, you may end up setting yourself up for future calamity. Always inquire of the Lord before you make the crucial decision of a marriage partner.

★ **Under pressure:** Pressure has led many people to early graves. People give in to pressure from peers and parents on a daily basis. Other kinds of pressure include: communal pressure, self-induced pressure, religious pressure, and the like.

A man told me how he was put under constant pressure by the pastor in his local assembly to get married. His pastor felt he was getting too old to remain single. Even though, deep in his heart he was not ready to shoulder the commitment and responsibility of marriage, his pastor insisted he needed to get married quickly because many young people in the church looked up to him for spiritual guidance.

This brother was very passionate about his church and wanted to keep serving, and the pressure he was put under by his pastor led him to get married to a lady without a proper courtship. Two years into the marriage, life became unbearable for the lady. The brother had no affection for or connection with her whatsoever. He treated her like a piece of furniture until she became fed up and left him. The news of their separation was all over the church and it affected his reputation and position in the church. He also forfeited the opportunity to pursue his passion of serving God in the local church.

Do not marry someone just because of pressure from people around you. Some parents nag their children into bad relationships and marriages because of their desire to have grandchildren. When you marry as a result of these pressures, none of the friends or family members who pressured you will share in the pain and disappointment that may ensue. There is a divine time for everyone, and trying to jump the divine queue may put you into more trouble in life. Patiently wait on God for your time and season because God's timing is always best. The Bible says in Ecclesiastes 3:11: "He hath made everything beautiful in his time..." It is always beautiful when you find love naturally without any pressure.

* By an alleged 'prophetic' word from a third party: We live in a generation where so many people lack the fear of God and yet claim to hear from God. Their desire, greed, flesh or mind speaks to them and they impose it on others as a word from the Lord. Some people become so obsessed about a guy or a lady to the point where their mind is full of fantasies about the person. They imagine their future together and desperately desire to get married to them. Soon, they will start seeing the object of their attention in their sleep. The dreams they have and other mind games they subject themselves to are mainly engineered by their desire to be in a relationship with the person. They usually misconstrue their desire to be the voice of God.

The Bible says in Ecclesiastes 5:3: "If you keep thinking about something, you will dream about it..." Some people are purely driven by lust and infatuation. They get so taken up by these emotions that they manufacture a self-induced prophetic word to lure innocent victims into their trap.

So many men and women are in miserable marriages and relationships today because they were deceived by an alleged prophecy to marry their spouses.

Years ago, I met a lady who was married with two children. She had been married to her husband for almost 10 years. One day, after an argument, her husband told her that he only married her because she said the Lord said he was her husband. Their relationship was full of misery and pain for many years until they invited God afresh into their marriage to fix the foundational error caused by the inability to differentiate between the voice of desire and the voice of God.

As a believer, when it comes to critical issues of life such as marriage, it is very important that you do not accept blindly an alleged prophetic word claiming that you are meant to be someone's husband or wife. It is important that you hear from God. The price Jesus paid on the cross granted us direct access to God without the need for any intermediary. God will not push you into a marriage for the rest of your life without informing you about it. At least, there has to be a confirmation in your spirit before you yield to someone's claim of receiving a prophetic word for you.

It is crucial that you know your walk with God is a relationship that makes God the first party and you the second party. Everyone else is a third party. Matters of destiny are crucial and should not be taken likely.

When I was single, I got a number of alleged prophetic words from sisters who claimed that the Lord said I was their future husband. These claims were contrary to what the Lord was saying to me and I had to politely dismiss them.

Many so-called prophets have joined people together in marriage backed by a supposed word from God. They do these things without even giving both parties involved the opportunity to pray or think about it. Some so-called prophets go as far as threatening parties with spiritual calamity if they hesitate to act in line with their so-called prophecy. Before you submit to a prophetic word from any third party, it is sensible that you pray about it and have a confirmation in your spirit before taking action.

In Jeremiah 29:30-31, the scripture speaks about false prophets who claim to speak in the name of the Lord when in reality they have heard nothing from God.

How to Discern the Right Man/Woman

As God's children we need to constantly remind ourselves that our steps are meant to be ordered by the Lord (Psalms 37:23). The Lord orders our steps by speaking to our spirit and instructing us on the actions we should take as we go through life's journey. God's voice is crucial to our destiny. Isaiah 30:21 declares, "Your ears shall hear a word behind you, saying, 'this is the way, walk in it,' whenever you turn to the right hand or whenever you turn to the left."

God is always eager to speak to us especially in the crucial areas of our lives. Unfortunately, many do not recognize the voice of God. Failure to recognize God's voice when he speaks may make us go astray in various aspects of our life. Therefore, to be able to discern the right man or woman for you, there is a great need to be able to recognize God's voice when He speaks to you.

Jesus spoke in John 10:27. He said, "My sheep hear my voice, and I know them, and they follow me." We are sheep in God's pasture and He speaks to us through the Holy Spirit.

When we spend quality time in God's presence, study His word and maintain constant communion with the Holy Spirit, we become familiar with God's voice to the point where we recognize it and can distinguish it from any other voice in and around us. Being able to hear God speak to us is one of the many benefits of being a child of God. A man or woman who hears from God and obeys is someone who will be able to sharply discern the right man or woman when the time to get married comes. Whenever we hear from God, we have peace in our hearts and we become very confident because we know deep within us that we have God's endorsement for the decision we are about to make.

Walking with and hearing from God is progressive and no matter your present spiritual level, you can always improve on your relationship with God. The more time you spend with God, the more of Him you know, and the more of Him you know, the better you will hear from Him. This will improve your chances of making the right marital choice.

Section 3

Chapter Seven
Question Time

One of my favourite programs on British television is a program on BBC One. The program, which is presented by David Dimbleby, is called **Question time.** During this program, politicians, government officials, cabinet members, members of parliaments and policy makers are invited to explain or defend their policies with a panel that consists of politicians and people with opposing views. The most interesting part of the program for me is when selected members of the public who form a live audience, are given the opportunity to ask questions. I have watched a number of episodes in which some questions from the live audience could not be answered by some panellists. On the other hand, there were other episodes where grilling questions aimed at destabilizing some panellists were cleverly answered to the point where their answers where applauded by the live audience.

At the end of the program, members of the public become more enlightened and members of the panel leave the studio with a good picture of what an average person thinks on a certain policy or on any matter of social interest.

As a single person, there is a need for you to have something similar in your life. Having a question time for yourself would help you evaluate your life and learn a lot about yourself. The difference between the **Question time** on British television and the one you need to put together as a single person is that instead of having a live audience and a panel consisting of various people, you will be the moderator, the panel and the live audience.

There are pertinent questions you need to ask yourself and answer sincerely. I personally believe that the greatest liar is the person that lies to him or herself. If we pause and evaluate our lives intermittently, we would prevent a lot of problems even before they surface.

As a single person there are some questions you need to ask yourself before you go into a relationship. The honest answers you give to these questions will present you with a good picture of who you are and what you really want out of a relationship. Below are some of the fundamental questions every single should ask and answer before considering a relationship:

Who Am I?

It is the desire of almost everyone to be understood by the person they are in a relationship with. We all want our spouses, fiancé, fiancées, family members and friends to know us better and it gives us joy when they do. However, the big question is how do you expect them to know and understand you when you do not even have a clue as to who you are? Knowing who you are will make it easier for others to get to know you.

Before you go into a relationship, you need to know what your purpose of existence is, and like I always say, there is more to life than marriage. You are not in this world just to get married, have kids, get old and die. You need to give your life a meaning by discovering yourself and your purpose.

Our lives are meant to touch other lives in a positive way, but this can only come to be when we know who we are.

The person you intend to be in a relationship with will relate with you better if you know who you are and what you stand for. Many singles today are neither here nor there; they have conflicting views and personalities because of an identity crisis resulting from not knowing for sure who they are. You will only end up complicating your love life if you do not know the answer to the above question.

Knowing who you are and what you stand for increases your confidence and gives you a sense of direction in life. It also makes the people that come your way aware of what you stand for and this removes a whole load of complication out of your relationships.

Do not allow other people to tell you who they think you are. You are the best person to answer this question. When you answer it convincingly, you will make life a lot easier for you and for the person you will be in a relationship with.

You were created by God for a reason. His thoughts and plans for you are great. Instead of wasting your life trying to be someone else, seek God and ask Him to reveal your purpose to you. By so doing, you will be on your way to knowing who you really are and why you are here.

What Do I Want?

If you don't know what you are searching for, how can you recognize it when you come across it? Many people desperately want to be in a relationship but they have no clue as to the kind of relationship they want or the kind of person they desire to be with. Failure to know what you want might leave you settling for something less than you can actually attain.

People who know what they want in a relationship and in life as a whole are usually focused and goal-oriented. If you walk into a car shop with the objective of buying a seven-seater car for your family that comprises of you, your wife and your four kids, you will not get to the car shop and start negotiating for a car with only two seats. No matter how hard the sales man tries to convince you about the benefits of such a car, you will not give in because you know what will and will not serve your purpose. The same applies to relationship issues. When you know who you are and what you want out of life, you will recognize the man or woman who can fit into your life.

This recognition makes you bother less about going into a relationship with someone heading in a direction different from where you are heading. Many singles go into relationships just for the fun of it. They know the relationship will not lead anywhere, yet they go into it just to be numbered among those who are said to be in a relationship.

The truth of the matter is that any relationship you go into will take something out of you. For this reason, you cannot afford to keep entering relationships that end up taking your time, energy and virtue for nothing.

I met a single lady some years ago in the city of London. She was hoping to get married and she knew exactly the kind of man she wanted. A responsible guy approached her, proposed to her and wanted to marry her. Many of her friends were astonished because the guy was considered by them to be rare gem; a man most women would desire to marry. However, she did not feel the same way, which made some of her friends think she was stupid to allow a golden opportunity pass her by.

I asked her why she was not interested in the guy and she simply told me, "This is not the kind of person I want and there is no confirmation in my spirit about him." I was so happy to hear that because she was someone who knew what she wanted out of life. The guy in question was rich and godly, but he was not the one for her.

Many men and women have rushed into relationships not because they love the other person, or he or she fits the description of what they want; they go into the relationship because the person meets the generic requirements. The generic qualities for so many ladies today are a man who is nice-looking, a good listener, godly, rich and romantic.

On the other hand, many men generally would want to go into a relationship with a lady who is beautiful, resourceful and faithful; someone who hardly nags. As good as all these qualities are, you cannot just settle with any man or woman that possesses them; you need to streamline your choice in line with your purpose and desires, subject to the endorsement of the Holy Spirit.

Before you dive into a relationship, it is very important you ask yourself this question: "Is this what I really want?" Do not go into a relationship just to pass time or feel comfortable in the midst of your friends who are already in relationships. Your time is very precious and you cannot afford to waste it. Wasting your time is as good as wasting your life.

When you know what you want out of life, stick to it. Your desires may not come at the time you want them to, but they will certainly come at their appointed time. Do not settle for less than what God has put in your heart. If you settle for "quick fix," the consequences might be damning.

This does not mean that you should be too picky or set unrealistic standards when it comes to choosing a life partner. It simply means that you should know what you want, go for it and settle for nothing less than what God has for you!

Am I ready & willing to pay the price?

Nothing good in life comes easy; there is always a price to pay. Something may be given to you free, but practically, it has to be paid for by someone else. We were saved freely by the finished work of Christ on the cross, but our salvation did not come cheap; Jesus paid the ultimate price for us with His life.

Your dreams hopes, aspirations, desires, needs and wants in life will not always come to you on a platter of gold; they will sometimes involve sacrifices. Even if you have a good picture of who you are and what you want out of life, there is no guarantee that everything will fall into place automatically. Many people start well in life, but become stranded midway into their journey because their dexterity wore off along the way. For every dream you have, there is a price.

The prices we pay for our desired future comes in various shapes and sizes. Things may be difficult along the way, but if we hold on tight, we will smile at the end of the day. Many people desire lovely relationships, however, these don't just happen. Good relationships are made over time.

My wife and I have been so blessed to have great mentors in our lives. Early in our relationships they made us understand this truth. We embraced it and constantly reminded ourselves of it when things became rough. Why give up on a great relationship just because of hard times? That God is in your relationship does not mean it will be totally void of challenges. As a matter of fact, godly marriages are more prone to attacks from the enemy because they are a testimony of God's handiwork; they are also units for the healing and transformation of society.

Are you willing to fight for your marriage and make it work? Are you willing to be called names just because you want to do things God's way? Are you willing to wait for longer than others might do in order to be in the right relationship? Are you willing to stick to your wedding vows even when things are hard? Are you willing to forgive even when it does not make sense? Your response to these questions will determine how far you are ready to go for the manifestation of what the Lord has in store for you.

It is not enough to know who you are and what you want. It is not even enough to know that God is with you. It is essential that you also make a firm decision to stay strong till the very end.

Chapter Eight

Six Important Questions You Need to Ask Yourself Before You Go Into a Relationship:

1. *Am I ready for a relationship?* There is no point going into a relationship when you are not ready for one. You have to be psychologically, spiritually, physically and financially ready for it. This readiness is not a function of age. It is possible to be old enough to marry and lack the psychological maturity that is needed in marriage. If you go into a relationship or marriage prematurely, you will end up frustrating yourself and the person you are in a relationship with. Wait until you are ready before you stir up love. Relationships are not for the weak, selfish, impatient or faint-hearted; they are for people who are prepared and ready to go all the way. The Bible says in the book of Songs of Solomon 8:4: "...don't excite love, don't stir it up, until the time is ripe and you are ready." Many singles have broken so many hearts and are themselves heartbroken because they got into something they were not prepared for. When you are ready for a relationship, you will be more committed and ready to handle the challenges that come along with it.

2. *Am I ready to make a commitment to one person?* We live in an era where total commitment to one relationship at a time is scarce. Many singles consciously go into serious

relationships with numerous people at the same time. I strongly believe that if you cannot commit to one relationship at a time as a single person, you may find it very difficult to stay committed and faithful to one woman or man when you eventually get married.

If you are thinking about starting a relationship, ask yourself this important question before you go ahead; and if your answer is "no", then it is better for you wait until you find the person you can love and stay committed to. Being committed to more than one relationship at a time makes you double-minded; it deprives you from fully investing and benefiting from any of them. No wonder the Bible says in James 1:8: "A double-minded man is unstable in all his ways."

What separates the men from the boys when it comes to relationships is that the men are ready to make a solid commitment while the boys still play around in the world of indecision. Wait until you are ready to make an unwavering commitment to a relationship before you go into one.

3. *Do I genuinely love this person?* What is the point of being in a relationship with someone you do not love? It is totally useless! Going into a relationship without love is like embarking on a long journey without petrol or diesel in your car. Love in a relationship is like the fuel that keeps a car moving. Unfortunately, so many relationships and marriages today are running on empty!

A relationship without love will eventually become a chore and it may end up in disaster. Don't just start a relationship because everyone around you is in one; you cannot fake love. You will know if it is in your relationship or not.

If your answer to the above question is "no" or "maybe"; if you cannot answer the question confidently, then pause and wait until you are 100 percent sure before you go into a relationship.

4. *Does this person love me genuinely for the right reasons?* It is one thing for someone to say they love you and it is another thing for them to love you for the right reasons. If you are not sure they love you, then there is no need to go into a serious relationship with them. However, if they say they do and you discover that they love you for the wrong reasons, then wisdom demands that you pause and ponder. If someone loves you only for what you have or what you can do, then that is not a genuine love. Genuine love is when you love someone just the way they are, with or without anything they seem to have.

When someone claims to love you, make sure you ascertain the claim. You will know from their actions if they are telling the truth. If you are in doubt, pause and seek God's face. He will reveal the truth to you.

5. *What is God saying about this relationship?* Wise people ask God before they make a commitment to somebody for life. The best time to involve God in your relationship is at the very beginning. If God is at the foundation of your relationship, it will stand the test of time.

Before you go into any relationship, enquire of the Lord to ascertain His will. God can only bless and preserve what He is a part of. If He is not part of it, He is not in it. Many people find it very hard to hear from God when it comes to their relationships, this is because they allow their emotions to lead the way. It is better to know what God is saying concerning your relationship at the beginning than to wait until you go through much pain and struggle before you go to Him for direction.

6. *What is his/her vision and purpose in life?* It is very crucial that you ask whoever you are about to start a serious relationship with the above question. A man or woman who

has no sense of direction in life will become a distraction and a liability to you if go into a serious relationship with him or her. Proverbs 29:18 says, "Where is no vision, the people perish…" It is not enough to be in love with someone; you also need to know where the relationship is heading and where parties to the relationship hope to be in the future. When you ask this question, the response you get will help you know where you are headed and how you can be of help to each other. Their answer will also reveal if you are heading in the same direction or not. No matter how much you want a relationship to work, if the person you are about to go into a relationship with is headed in the opposite direction, you need to pause and end the relationship.

It is better that you ask yourself and the person you intend to go into a relationship with these crucial questions that will determine if they are capable and ready to embark on the journey of life with you. Ask these questions at the very start of the relationship in order not to waste your precious time. Your time is your life and your life is your time. Cherish it!

Chapter Nine
Questionable Relationships

M any singles get themselves emotionally involved in relationships that they fail to examine. They fail to see glaring signs that the relationship is questionable. Although there is no such thing as a "perfect relationship", it is very important you take note of things that show that the relationship you are in is dubious.

Ideally, there should be a place for reasoning, emotions and discernment in every relationship. Unfortunately, many people ignore the voice of reason and discernment, and allow their emotions to be the major force that drives the relationship. If you assess your relationship with the lens of emotions alone, you are bound to skip important details and warning signals.

There are signs that always show up when you, as a child of God, are in a relationship that is questionable. It is very important that you don't waste your time and life in the face of glaring signs indicating that the future of the relationship is in doubt.

Let us look at some signs that could indicate you are in a questionable relationship:

• Secrecy: Are you in a relationship with someone for a reasonable period of time yet they refuse to disclose the relationship to the people around them? It is very likely that are you are in a questionable relationship. I have said this several times: love is a beautiful thing and you should be happy and proud to tell the people around you that you are in a relationship.

• Constant procrastination: Beware of people who constantly procrastinate about their intentions towards you and the relationship. Some people keep talking about taking you to meet their parents/friends, or taking practical steps to move the relationship to the next serious level, but they never act on their word.

A guy kept a girl in limbo for almost ten years. He kept on procrastinating about his intentions to engage and marry her from the second year they dated until the tenth. He wasted her time and life and at the end of the day, he snuck away and married someone else, leaving the lady confused and heartbroken. True love is a force that propels us to action.

Some people use procrastination to buy their way out of a relationship. They keep blowing hot and cold intermittently, sending conflicting signals to the person they are in a relationship with. Are you single? Be very mindful of people who do not love you enough to take you seriously; people who want to keep sitting on the fence for selfish reasons.

• Absence of Spiritual Guidance: As a single Christian in a relationship, it is wise to have spiritual guidance. If you are in a relationship with a person who claims to love you and wants to marry you, but is hesitating to see your spiritual leader, then you have to be careful. Regardless of the size of your church, when you are about to take a vital step such as getting married; your team leader, cell group leader, pastor, etc. can offer you sound advice. If you are in a relationship with someone who barks at the idea of meeting your spiritual head, you should closely examine their intentions.

•   Absence of the fear of God: A relationship void of the fear of God is really questionable. How far can you go without God? What future do you hope to build without the fear of God? The scripture says that the fear of the Lord is the beginning of wisdom. Without the fear of God, sexual sins, lying, cheating, deception and other ungodly acts can easily become the norm. The fear of the Lord enables us to honour God in our relationships and live a holy life. Godly relationships draw you closer to God, not the opposite.

•   Lack of internal peace: As a child of God, even if you are in a relationship that is approved by everyone around you and yet you have no peace about it, then like we said earlier, you may be in a questionable relationship. If as a single person, you are in a relationship void of peace in your heart, pause and seek God's face so He can speak to you clearly about the relationship.

As a single person if at anytime or stage in your relationship you discover that you are in a questionable relationship don't just sit back and do nothing; ask the Lord to speak to you and He will show you things as they really are. Don't just stay put in a disastrous relationship because of the fear of what people might say or think about you.

Abraham A Jones

Section 4

Chapter Ten
Kingdom Relationships

Current statistics in the United Kingdom show that 71.6 percent of its inhabitants claim to be Christians. In other words, the United Kingdom can be said to be a Christian nation. Unfortunately, the percentage of people that regularly attend church is less than 11 percent. Imagine the impact Christians in the United Kingdom would make in Europe and all over the world if all 71.6 percent of them decided to actively apply godly, kingdom principles in their relationships, marriages and lives.

As a believer, you are a child of God and you belong to a kingdom whose King is Jehovah. In this kingdom, things are not done anyhow; they are done in ways that are consistent with the principles of the kingdom.

There are values that should guide people who intend to pursue a serious relationship with each other. We serve a God of order and He would not just leave us to do things in a chaotic way. Since we serve a God of order, we ought to do things in a way that reflects the kingdom-lifestyle we were called to live.

Although marriages are failing in their hundreds on a daily basis across the globe, we ought to stand out and show good examples worthy of emulation. Unfortunately, that has not been the case. Many Christian marriages are suffering worse fates compared to their non-Christian counterparts. These days, people even find it hard to tell the difference between a Christian marriage and a non-Christian marriage because many are trending towards the direction of the world. With almost 50 percent of marriages failing in some countries today, believers need to rise up and stand out positively by faithfully applying kingdom principles in their relationships.

We are ambassadors of God's kingdom here on earth. We need, therefore, to replicate the kingdom lifestyle wherever we find ourselves. Luke 17:21 says, "No one will say 'look, here it is!' or there it is!' because the kingdom of God is within you." God's presence is not just in a church building; it is within us because we are His temple; His dwelling place. This understanding will keep us conscious of who we are, where we are coming from and why we are here.

We live in an era where the purpose of relationships and marriage are misunderstood and abused by so many people. It is often said that if the purpose of a thing is not known, abuse is inevitable. How true! Whenever you are in doubt about the purpose of a thing, it is better you refer to the inventor the thing. Marriage was not created by man; it was created by God. Therefore, to understand its purpose, we need to refer to Him for guidance.

Many look up to Hollywood, science and human intelligence to see success in their relationships and marriages, but instead of the relationships working, they have been getting even worse. Clearly, the world does not have the answers; the answers are in the hand of the Creator. We need to go back to the very beginning and retrace our steps. The genesis of marriage is found in God's word. Success at this God-originated institution, therefore, cannot be without Him.

What is the purpose of relationships and marriage? Why did God bother to create this ancient institution? We will soon explore the answers to these questions. It is very important we know, however, that marriage is not just for having sex and for procreation. There is more to it than all that.

Let us quickly look at the qualities of a kingdom-relationship as God intended from the very beginning in Genesis chapter two:

Foundation:

The foundation of your relationship is very important. It determines the strength, duration, condition and the end of your relationship. The foundation of a kingdom relationship should be God. Failure to make God the pillar of your future home can be likened to building an expensive house on sandy ground. Regardless of the costly materials you use in building the house, it will not stand for long.

The initiator of marriage is God, and if we are to succeed in our relationships, we have to make Him our sole foundation. Any foundation other God is just a temporal fix with no guarantees.

Marriage is God's idea. In Genesis 2:18-25 God facilitated the first wedding in creation between Adam and Eve. Do not build your home on anything other than the One who created the institution.

In Genesis chapter sixteen, Abraham was pressured into having a relationship with Hagar, Sarah's maid. This relationship was not approved by God and as a result it did not have God's blessing. It ended badly because God was not a part of it. God always protects what He is part of. The relationship between Hagar and Abraham was contrary to the promises and instructions he received from God concerning him and Sarah.

People that do things God's way always have God's divine intervention in times of trouble. A godly foundation gives birth to a godly relationship. Building a relationship on an ungodly foundation always results in a negative outcome. Some of these consequences may end up being generational as seen in the life of King David in the Bible. King David killed Uriah, one of his soldiers, so he could marry his wife, Bath-Sheba. This relationship was built on a bloody foundation and it later had a generational effect on his family.

Some of the generational effects of King David's sexual sins included King Solomon, who ended up with seven hundred wives and three hundred concubines (1 Kings 11:3); the defiling of King David's wives by his son Absalom (2 Samuel 16:22); and the defiling of King David's daughter (Tamar) by her brother (Amnon)(2 Samuel 13:14).

So many people are suffering today as a result of a faulty foundation. Save yourself and your future generation from troubles that may arise as a result of building on the wrong foundation.

Companionship:

Not every friend or person around you can understand you to the point where they can be your wife or husband. In Genesis chapter two, before Eve came on to the scene, Adam was surrounded by many other creatures that God created, but he could not relate on the same frequency with any of them. God saw the need to create a companion that could interact with Adam on the same frequency of spirit, soul and body.

Are you currently in a relationship or hope to be in one? It is very important that your future spouse understand you enough to be a companion. Relationships are not just about going out on dates, parties or other social functions; they are about understanding each other. Do they understand you, your calling, your purpose and your personality? Are they willing to really know you? I am not talking about a fair-weather companion; I am referring to someone who would stand with you through good and bad times. Relationships and marriages end quickly today because parties are in them for the good times only.

One of the sad things that can happen to anyone in a relationship or marriage is feeling alone in that relationship. This can happen as a result of a lack of understanding from the person someone is in a relationship with. Do you feel alone even though you are in a serious relationship? Do you feel as if there is no synergy between you and the person you are relating with? Pause and pray. Seek God's face for wisdom on what to do. Amos 3:3 says, "Can two walk together, except they be agreed?" Without understanding, there can be no agreement, and without agreement you cannot build a loving kingdom relationship that will stand the test of time.

The companion you choose for the journey of life can determine if the journey will be sweet or bitter. That is why the scripture says in Proverbs 13:20: "He that walks with the wise, shall be wise, but a companion of fools shall be destroyed." May God give you wisdom to choose the right companion.

Suitability:

Verse 18 of Genesis 2 reveals God's decision to make a "helper suitable for Adam." As a single person, not every "helper" around you is suitable for you. Many people have ended up marrying people just because they were supported and helped by them at various points in their lives. Your life and future is too important to give away to someone just because they helped you in life.

The helper you require in life has to be "suitable" for you. The person needs to suit your calling and assignment. Marrying the wrong helper may destroy your future. Being in a relationship with someone who does not suit you is being unequally yoked; so many people are unequally yoked in their relationships. Do not be yoked with someone who will hinder or slow you down in the journey of life, instead seek the Lord's face and He will help you choose a suitable helper. He alone can reveal your suitable helper to you.

Suitable helpers will make your relationship and marriage a sweet experience, even in the midst of challenges. I know many people who went contrary to God's word in 2 Corinthians 6:4; they got themselves yoked to people who later hindered them from maximizing their potential and fulfilling their purposes in life.

Positive Confessions:

We are gods on this earth. We represent God Himself and our words are very powerful. Jesus said in John 6:63: "...the words I speak to you, they are spirit and they are life." Our words frame our world. In verse 19 of Genesis 2, the Lord gave Adam the power to name all the beast of the field and all the fowls of the air, and whatever name Adam called them automatically became their name. Parties to a kingdom relationship will speak life into each other; they will stand in the place of prayer and address their situation, calling it what God wants it to be. Even if you are married to God's will for your life, challenges will still come your way. Do not allow these challenges to push you out of your God-given relationship. Speak life into your situation by using God's word.

Death and life are sealed on our lips and it is our choice to either speak life or death. Speak life into you future spouse, your life and your relationship, and with time you will begin to see positive manifestations in and around you.

Total Submission to God:

In verse 21 of Genesis 2, the scripture tells us that the Lord caused a deep sleep to fall upon Adam before one of his ribs was taken to create Eve. Why did the Lord put Adam in a state of sleep? So he would not interfere with what He was about to do. The state of sleep signified a state of total surrender and submission to God's will.

Today, doctors use anaesthetics to make patients lose sensation and consciousness so they can perform effective surgeries. In order for you to fully enjoy your relationship, you need to be in total surrender and submission to God's will. Many people have interfered with God's plan for their lives because they thought they knew what they needed in their relationship-life. From choosing a life partner to building a godly family, we need to be in total submission to God's will.

God knows what is best for us. He knows the end from the beginning. It is better we trust and submit to Him rather than depend on our intellect or experience.

A relationship that is under God's supervision and authority stands a better chance of succeeding, much more so than the one that is under the supervision of man's wisdom. Also, a relationship that is totally submitted to God will be surrounded by less demonic activities. Resisting the devil becomes very easy when your relationship is totally submitted to God's authority. No wonder the scripture says in James 4:7: "Submit yourself therefore to God. Resist the devil, and he will flee from you."

Equality:

Verses 21-23 of Genesis 2 make it very clear that the Lord took a rib from Adam's side. He did not take a bone from his back, leg or hand. He intentionally took it from his side. This signifies that the woman was designed to stand side-by-side with man.

Many women are put behind the man and treated like second-class citizens in today's society and in their homes. In the realm of the spirit, however, there is no gender. Discriminating between genders is, therefore, baseless and ungodly. In a kingdom relationship, parties see themselves as co-equals and although the man is the head of the home, he is not better than the woman and vice versa.

The human rib cage is so important. It protects one of the most vital organs in our body; the heart. Our heart is the vital organ that pumps blood to the whole body; without a rib cage, the heart would easily suffer damage from minor impacts.

God designed woman with the special grace to protect a man's heart and bring life to him in many ways. If you find the right woman, she will be a blessing to you beyond words. However, the wrong woman can end your life abruptly.

A kingdom relationship is one where parties see each other as equal partners fulfilling different roles in order to achieve a common goal. It is expedient that you treat the person you are in a relationship with respectfully. If you see yourselves as equal, you will treat each other nicely – in the same way you would want to be treated.

Communication:

A relationship void of healthy communication is a relationship that is heading nowhere. When Adam awoke from his deep sleep in Genesis 2:23, upon seeing Eve, the first thing he did was to speak. Communication is vital, and in order for a relationship to flourish, parties in it must communicate with each other in a healthy way. Communication can be verbal or non-verbal, and can be carried out in a healthy manner or in an unhealthy manner. It is not enough to talk to the person you are in a relationship with; you need to talk to him/her with respect.

As human beings we naturally switch off our attentiveness when someone is communicating with us in a rude manner. Many couples talk to each other, but they do not enjoy the benefits of healthy communication.

Communication enables you to share your heart, fears, hopes and dreams with the person you love. Communication increases the bond between parties in a loving relationship. It is a key quality of a kingdom relationship. Relationships void of communication are most likely going to fall apart over time.

Transparency:

A relationship void of transparency is a relationship that is heading nowhere. Transparency increases trust and a kingdom relationship is a relationship built on trust. In verse 25 of Genesis 2, the Bible says: "And they were both naked, the man and his wife, and were not ashamed." This scripture is so profound because it wasn't just talking about physical nakedness; it also implied that there were no secrets between them. Everything was bare for both of them to see.

In a kingdom relationship, couples are open and transparent with each other. Their strengths and weaknesses are bare and they are not ashamed of them. Falling in love with the right person is a very beautiful thing, because the right person will accept you just as you are. Regardless of your imperfections, excesses and areas that need improvement, their love for you will remain constant.

There are no secrets between parties in a kingdom relationship. They operate a transparent policy and are honest about their past, finances, fears, hopes, dreams and lives. The one person you should never hide, pretend to or deceive is the person you claim to love. True love is void of ambiguity; it is straight and plain.

Chapter Eleven

Kingdom Parameters In Relationships

A lthough Jesus' death on the cross of Calvary set us free, the freedom is not a license for us to do whatever we please. Rather, the freedom is within the confines of God's word. A kingdom without principles is a kingdom that will soon experience a decline. So many young believers go about proclaiming their freedom in Christ, but forget that this freedom comes with both benefits and responsibilities. Our works did not procure our salvation; we are required to walk with God in order to continue enjoying and maximizing it in Christ.

Proverbs 29:18 says: "Where there is no revelation, the people cast off restraints; but happy is he who keeps the law." A lack of revelation makes many single Christians think they can do anything they like in their relationships, even if what they do contradicts God's word. God's word is very clear on every aspect of our relationships, and as kingdom ambassadors, we ought to be different. We cannot adopt the ways of the world. Everything we do has to be in line with God's principles.

Let us take a look at the kingdom parameters in relation to dating, friendship and courtships, the very ways God intended for them to be:

Dating

The word 'dating', usually, is used in reference to the meeting of two people in a mutually agreed place for social activity or other functions. People who go on dates usually do so with the aim of assessing each other's suitability as a spouse. Millions of young and old people across the world go on dates on a daily basis.

The opinions that people have on dating vary from place to place; nonetheless, the idea is a fast-growing phenomenon amongst young people today. Many parents are so busy doing their thing that they have no clue as to what their kids are up to. These days, teens go on dates with total strangers without the knowledge of their parents or guardians. Many end up being molested and abused in the process because they had no one to give them guidelines or help them when they prepared to go on dates.

Are you a parent? Just because you do not see your children going on dates does not mean that they are not doing so. They are probably simply not telling you. It is imperative therefore, that you educate and equip them so as to prevent them from falling into the snare of the evil one.

I always tell Christian singles who go on dates that the value they place on themselves will most likely be the value their date will place on them. If you are on a date and you do not place value upon yourself, do not be surprised when your date treats you cheaply. In the world, many go on their first date and begin to have sex; they engage in other things that are only legitimate for married couples. If you give your body to a man or a woman on your first date, what message are you passing on to him or her?

In 1 Corinthians 6:19-20 we are made us to understand that our body is the temple of God and we have been bought with a price — the precious blood of Jesus. We do not own ourselves; we belong to God. If we truly belong to God and

He lives in us, why would we want to defile His dwelling place? We were bought with the precious blood of the Lamb and that is not cheap!

I always advise people going on dates, especially when meeting their date for the first time, to take note of the following:

➢ Let your meeting be in a public place; this is a wise action that can ensure your safety. Meeting people in unsafe places may jeopardize your safety and may make some people take undue advantage of you.

➢ Kissing and inappropriate touching should be avoided during dating. These defile God's temple and portray you as someone who is desperate and cheap.

➢ Always inform a third party about the date. Let the person know who you are going out with and where you are going; this is a common sense approach that has preserved people's lives.

➢ Try as much as possible not to stay out too late, especially on your first date. Evil prevails faster in the dark. Try to keep your date within godly hours so you can return home in good time.

➢ During your date, ask intelligent questions in order to assess the intention, honesty and personality of your date.

➢ Do not give too much personal information away on your first date and at the early stage of your relationship. You need to discern his or her intention and commitment before you start giving a lot away.

➢ While on a date, do not be too carried away by the ambience and personality of your date. Ask the Lord to reveal their true identity to you.

➢ Do not sleep over at your date's house. It is a clear opportunity for the enemy to ruin your testimony. Do not give the enemy a chance to make you fall into sexual sin.

➤ If, by chance, anything unpleasant happens to you during your date or if your date takes undue advantage of you, do not keep it to yourself. Instead, speak out and reach out to someone for help.

➤ Be civil and respect yourself.

Friendship

Some single people go on dates with people they are already friends with and some agree to dates with people they have never met. Whatever the case, it is important to be friends with the person you hope to spend the rest of your life with.

Basically, there are two types of friendships: Affectionate and personal regard. Affectionate friendship is when we develop a liking for someone of the opposite sex with the hope of being in a serious relationship with him or her, leading to marriage. On the other hand, friends under personal regard are normal friends in our lives without any romantic or affectionate attachment. Friends from our communities, schools, groups, work colleagues, etc. fall under this second category; they are people you have a personal regard for without any romantic strings attached.

It is expedient that you are friends with the person you intend to spend the rest of your life with. The length of your friendship can sometimes determine the strength of the bond between you and the person you are in a relationship with. This strong bond does not automatically eliminate disagreements, but it gives parties the opportunity to know each other to a certain degree.

There are many advantages in knowing and being friends with the person you are in a relationship with, some of these are listed below:

➤ Easy communication

- ➤ Stronger bond

- ➤ Increased trust

- ➤ Speedy conflict resolution

- ➤ Unity against external opposition

- ➤ Freely pray and seek God's face in times of trouble

- ➤ Easier to discuss futuristic plans

- ➤ Free flow of ideas, concerns, fears, etc.

Sometimes, a serious, romantic and affectionate relationship may eventually develop between two single people who were just friends with a personal regard for each other. There are some things you should note if you find yourself in this situation:

➤ Try not to get into a relationship with your close friend's ex; it ruins friendships.

➤ Do not accept or tolerate passes or flirty gestures from your friend's boyfriend/girlfriend or fiancé/fiancée.

These two points may not be laws carved on stone, but if you abide by them, they will earn you respect and dignity among your friends.

Courtship

A courtship is a serious stage in a relationship between a man and a woman who intend to spend the rest of their lives together; it is a period that precedes engagement and marriage.

Depending on the culture and orientation of people in courtship, as well as the influence they are under, the time of courtship may be a formal period known to and supervised by the respective families, or it may be a matter mainly between the man and the woman in question and anyone they choose to make the courtship known to. Courtship is a period where parties involved decide to take their relationship to a new level, ultimately leading to marriage. This is a very critical phase of a relationship and what transpires at this phase can determine if the relationship will succeed or fail.

Courtship is meant to be a time where the man and the woman engage and interact with each other intellectually, spiritually and financially, as they plan a future together. It is a time where the people in courtship are open and transparent to each other concerning matters that revolve around the wellbeing and the future of their relationship.

There is no stipulated duration to a courtship. It can vary from person to person. The society in which parties courting find themselves can also determine the length of courtship. Some people have a lengthy courtship, while others have a short one. Regardless of the duration, I always advise parties in a relationship that they should know fundamental things about each other before they get married.

Christian courtships differ from secular courtships. Christian courtships are meant to carry the mark of Christ from inception to conclusion. God's light should always shine in our lives and in our relationships. By so doing, we are setting a good example worthy of emulation for the people around us.

There are things people in Christian courtships should know. I will share just a few:

➢ Ask key questions: Parties in courtship should direct key questions at each other; questions that pertain to the vision, dreams, purpose and expectations of the person they are courting. They also need to share their hearts by talking about their strengths, limitations and challenges. They should be real and honest with each other about anything in their past, present or future that each of them needs to know.

Failure to disclose important information to the person you intend to marry may jeopardize the wellbeing of the relationship in the future.

➤ Do not court anyone in the dark: Beware of people who want you to have a secret courtship with them. If you are genuinely in love, you will be eager to share the news with the people in your life. Courting someone in the dark may expose you to people whose aim is to take undue advantage of you. Even in the case of extreme opposition to a relationship from third parties, it is very important that key people in your life, like your family, minister, or close friends, are aware of the fact that you are courting someone. If anyone approaches you with the intention of going into a secret relationship with you, chances are they have a hidden agenda. Prayerfully beware!

➤ Sexual purity: Hebrews 13:4 counsels us in this matter: "Marriage is honourable among all, and the bed undefiled; but fornicators and adulterers God will judge." Sexual purity during courtship is very important. It goes a long way to show your love and respect for God. When we honour God in our relationships, He will honour us in return. Most people are quick to assume that just because they are in a courtship or are engaged to be married, they have the right to engage in sexual activities. No! The scripture is clear on this matter. No matter how tempting and difficult it may be to restrain yourself from sexual immorality, when you depend upon the power of the Holy Spirit, He will make the impossible very possible for you.

➤ You should only court one person at a time.

➤ God must be at the centre of your courtship: failure to put God at the centre of your relationship may leave you stranded in the days of trouble. The presence of God gives you an edge when trouble comes.

➤ Spiritual investments: The courtship period is a very good time to invest spiritually in your relationship. Engage in prayer, fasting and spiritual activities that would strengthen your future home. Buy spiritual books, DVD's and CD'S; attend conferences, seminars and events that will help you develop spiritually.

➤ Be yourself: Do not pretend to be someone else just to impress people. Pretending to be someone else in courtship will set you up for failure. Be yourself and your intended partner will love you just the way you are.

➤ Do not fake it: If you are in a courtship and you later discover that it is not going to work out for some fundamental reasons, then you do not have to pretend. For the fear of what people might say or the fact that they spent many years in courtship, some people would rather fake their way into marriage than face reality. It is a very dangerous thing to do. A broken courtship is better than a broken marriage. If your courtship is not working and both parties in the courtship are not willing to work towards fixing it, then instead of faking it, leave it!

➤ Do not be blackmailed into courtship. It should be done out of free will.

➤ Faithfulness is not just to be practiced in marriage; it starts before marriage during courtship. Be faithful to the person you are courting.

➤ Constantly remind yourself of the fact that marriage is for life and honestly consider if you are able to commit to the person you are courting for life.

May your courtship be sweet and may your marriage be even sweeter in Jesus' name!

Chapter Twelve

Honesty In Relationships

It is always disturbing when I see seemingly good relationships go bad. One moment, you see a man and a woman madly in "love" with each other, and the next moment they begin to say the most horrible things about each other, causing the relationship to go down the drain. The question that comes to mind is, were they ever in love?

The above scenario was once rare in the Church, but today, it seems to be rampant. Some pastors now use the church as a match-making centre, offering candidates to the highest bidder. Some brothers in church also have come to perfect the act of swindling sisters, while some sisters have made a sport of sleeping around, not only with outsiders, but also with members and leaders of the church. Thereafter, they mix with the brethren to lift 'holy' hands. God cannot be mocked!

The word "love" is misunderstood by many today. Some people say, "I love you" but what they really mean by that is "I want you" or "I want to sleep with you." No wonder the divorce rate is on the rise.

Why would you want to be in a relationship that is heading nowhere? Why waste your precious time with a tongue-speaking player? Why hang on to someone who is only using you as a ladder to his or her selfish aims? In my years of counselling singles, I have come across a lot of people who wasted precious years of their lives just because they failed to be honest with each other at first.

Before and during your relationship, do not just be logical or emotional. Depending on your logic or emotions alone can be misleading. Your logic can fail you. Learn to use discernment and you will see beyond what is obviously in front of you.

It is very important that we embrace truth in any relationship we find ourselves in. Failure to be honest can cause you or the person you are in a relationship with so much pain. The good thing about honesty is that even if the relationship does not work out for some reason or the other, you can walk with your head up high for being honest. So many people cannot look at their ex-wives, husbands, boyfriends or girlfriends straight in the eye; they avoid them. Even if they meet up accidentally in the shopping mall or at a social gathering, they still avoid them because they were not honest when they were still relating. Do not be comfortable with lying to the person you claim to love. Where true love exists, everything is open and above board.

Ten Things You Need to Know Before You Say "I Do"

Ignorance and disobedience has made many people spend half their lifetime solving a problem they shouldn't have had in the first place. Before you practice law, you have to go to law school, and before you practice medicine, you have to go to medical school. These places of learning prepare and equip you for the task ahead. The thing about these and other professions is that you can retire after a certain number of years in service. Unfortunately, people rush into marriage without adequate preparation, and considering that marriage is designed to last for life, parties should be aware of what they are about to step into.

Do you desire to get married? Equip yourself with the relevant knowledge and information so your marriage can stand the test of time, because every marriage will pass through seasons of tests and challenges.

Below are ten vital things you need to know before you say "I do" to any man or woman:

1) Your Spouse is meant to 'complement you' and not 'complete you' as many assume. An insecure/incomplete single would be an insecure/incomplete spouse. Walk, therefore, to the marriage altar a complete person (Genesis 2:18).

2) Your single days are days of self-discovery and exploration. We all have a unique purpose; find yours and fulfil it (1 Corinthians 7:32-33).

3) Sex is a mystery. You leave a part of you in every person you have sexual intercourse with; spirits are transferred during sexual intercourse. In the light of this truth, premarital sex is not wise.

4) Your body does not belong to you. You have been bought with a price and there are consequences anytime you abuse your body, which is God's temple (1 Corinthians 3:16-17).

5) One of the best ways to know if your future wife or husband will be faithful to you is to see how honest and faithful they are to the Lord.

6) The foundation of your relationship will determine how well and how long it will last. No matter how spiritual you are, building on the wrong foundation is dangerous (Psalm 11:3).

7) There is no such thing as absolute autonomy or independence in marriage. Marriage is a partnership where

consultation is the order of the day. You cannot always do things your way in a marriage (Ephesians 5:21-25; 1 Corinthians 11:11).

8) There is more to life than marriage. Your ultimate purpose in life is not marriage. Marriage may help you fulfil your purpose, but it is not your sole purpose. Get a life and live it to the full (Ecclesiastes 12:13).

9) Marriage is an institution created and backed by God. We live in a world where people tend to make marriage look obsolete. Marriage is a covenant endorsed by heaven, do not take it lightly (Genesis 2).

10) Divorce was never God's plan. People go for the divorce option quickly these days. Marriage, however, is for good and hard times, and not just for good times. In a situation where there is violence or infidelity, parties should speak out and seek help from reliable sources before making a decision that will affect the future of their relationship.

NOTE: A wise man will not lift a finger against a woman and a wise woman has control over her tongue.

Abraham A Jones

Section 5

Chapter Thirteen
Along The Way

S everal years ago as a young lad, one of my elder brothers gave me his brand new car to go on an errand. I was fascinated by the car and could not wait to go on the trip.

I started the journey in the morning at about 9:00 am and I had a lovely drive to my place of assignment. After completing the mission, I started to make my way back to my brother's house. The arrangement was for me to pick his kids up from school on the way back. Half way to my brother's house, driving at about 70 miles per hour on the motorway, I heard a loud noise emanating from the car and it began to swerve to the left and to the right. After what seemed like hours, the car finally stopped. I got out only to discover that the front wheel was missing. It fell off.

Fellow drivers who saw what happened stopped by to congratulate me for cheating death in a remarkable way. To this day I still thank God for delivering me from the jaws of death.

The amusing thing, however, was that the car was brand new, straight from the factory! It was less than 3 weeks old. What could have gone wrong? How did it happen? These were the questions on my mind. Although I was grateful to be alive, I was also frustrated because I could not make my appointments for the day. It dawned on me that in life's journey, unexpected things do happen along the way.

People start a relationship with everything figured out perfectly. They are full of hope, excitement, energy and optimism. They work towards their dreams and aspirations in life only for them to be delayed or stopped in their tracks by unexpected events. The way we handle disappointments, challenges or delays in life vary from relationship to relationship and from person to person. They also go a long way to determine how well we go through life.

Many people end up with depression, bitterness, resentment and unforgiveness because of the unexpected things they encounter in their relationships and along the journey of life. In order to prevent such negative responses to the unexpected occurrences in relationships, let us take a look at some things that can help you along the way:

Conflict Resolution:

The early stages of marriage can give you an impression that you will never have a disagreement with your partner; you feel as though he or she understands you more than anyone else in the world. You feel an ocean of love for him or her, so much so that you think there is no way in a million years this feeling can ever be affected. The truth is that sometimes in life, the people we love the most end up annoying us the most.

Due to different backgrounds, ideologies and personalities, we mistakenly do and say things that may annoy or hurt the person we love. Every relationship has its challenges and conflicts, but the way we handle these challenges can strengthen or break the relationship.

Conflicts arise mainly as a result of disagreements, and a disagreement is the result of having a contrary view on a matter. Having a conflict in your relationship does not necessarily mean that the relationship was not meant to be or that the relationship is doomed. It is only the manifestation of a difference in perspective.

The best way to deal with conflict s is to resolve them. Do not leave conflicts unresolved between you and the person you love. Do not allow them to linger. The more they linger, the more damage they will cause your relationship.

However, the way you go about resolving a conflict matters a lot, it can deepen the conflict if it is addressed the wrong way. The question is: how do we go about resolving conflicts? Besides prayer, there are practical steps you can take that can turn a situation of conflict around positively. Let us quickly take a look at some:

Healthy Dialogue: It is not enough to initiate a peace-talk; it has to be done properly. When resolving a conflict through the conduit of dialogue, it is very important to realize that dialogue involves speaking *and* listening. Many people are eager to speak their minds, but they rarely allow the other party to voice their mind too. To properly resolve a conflict, both parties should have a say and talk things through it in the best way possible. To get maximum results when resolving a conflict through dialogue, there are some things you should consider:

1. Place of Dialogue: The place you choose to have your dialogue should be where both parties are comfortable. Choosing a place that suits only one party may make the other party unwilling to talk.

2. How You Talk: Your tone, pitch, choice of words and body language can determine if the other party gives you their maximum attention and cooperation or not. Be civil

and calm, use the right words to pass your message across, words that do not cause more damage to the situation.

3. Timing: The time you choose to resolve a conflict matters. Do not choose a time when the other party is stressed, tired or angry. Choose a time when you can get maximum participation and attention.

Seek Mediation: If you are unable to resolve a conflict by yourselves, it is important to seek mediation from someone who can be of help. Mediation is very good for both single and married people. It can go a long way toward pointing out things each party cannot see about the situation. In seeking mediation, it is crucial that both parties are in agreement as to who will carry out the mediation. It has to be a person both parties trust and respect. Go to a mediator that would not be biased; someone who will be fair and impartial to both of you.

Be Considerate: Sometimes the best way to resolve a conflict is to consciously be considerate of the person you are in a relationship with. Put yourself in their shoes before you do or say things that may offend them. When you see the person you love as part of you, it becomes easier to be considerate towards them.

Compromise: "Compromise" is a word you will have to embrace if you want to be in a relationship that will stand the test of time. You cannot always have your way. Remember, it is not just about you anymore. The moment you let someone into your life and heart, you will have to allow them to make decisions too, especially in the areas of their strengths. Relationship is a partnership where two people have equal say and stake. Do not assume or expect things to be done your way all the time. Sometimes, you have to compromise for the sake of love.

Accept and Celebrate Your Uniqueness: Many conflicts emanate from personal differences. Understanding

this fact will go a long way towards harmony and making the most of the differences between you and the person you are in a relationship with. By so doing, you will be saving yourself needless trouble that may emanate from trying to change the person you love to fit your mould.

Chapter Fourteen

Heartbreaks:

Heartbreaks are some of the things that can happen along the way, and as a single person you need to know a few things about heartbreak. Heartbreaks are emotional pains we experience; they can be caused by a host of reasons. We are particularly interested in heartbreaks that emanate from romantic relationships between singles of the opposite sex.

I strongly believe that over 70 percent of relationship heartbreaks that single people go through are preventable. However, there are times when heartbreaks occur for unavoidable reasons.

It is not unusual that people experience both pleasant and unpleasant relationships before they meet the right person. It is necessary, therefore, to know how to overcome the effects of heartbreaks if you ever encounter it as a single person.

The inability to prevent or overcome the effects of a relationship breakdown has led many to early graves and trapped others in depression, anger, bitterness, unforgiveness, low self-esteem, etc.

Some people say, "People learn from painful experiences in life." As true this statement may be, some painful experiences are totally unnecessary.

In my years of counselling singles, I discovered a few basic reasons why some singles experience a preventable heartbreak:

~~ Deadly Assumptions: It is very dangerous to assume to be in a relationship when in reality, the party you believe you are in a loving relationship with, only sees you as a friend.

Don't assume someone is interested in you or in love with you just because they smile at you all the time. Just because someone is kind and generous towards you does not automatically mean that they are interested in having a serious relationship with you. A loving relationship is a serious and powerful thing. Parties to it must not just assume they are in love; they need to *know* they are in love. There has to be clear and verbal communication between the parties involved. Until someone opens their mouth and tells you in clear terms how they feel about you, making assumptions that they love you may only lead you down Heartbreak Lane, especially when you eventually see them pursuing a serious relationship with someone else. It is not enough to assume someone loves you just because they hang out with you occasionally or regularly. I always say to singles that if they feel a fellow single of the opposite sex is getting too close to them, it is better they face the embarrassment of asking the person to be clear on their intentions with them than for them to assume something that does not exist.

~~ Concealed Relationships: If someone asks you into a relationship with him or her, and the person instructs you not to inform anyone about it, you could be heading for heartbreak. Over 97 percent of concealed relationships always end up in one form of disaster or another. Most people that do not want anyone to know they are in a relationship with you often have a hidden agenda. If you attend a church where someone claims to be in love with you and hopes to build a future with you, they should not hide it. Love is a beautiful thing to be celebrated not concealed.

Ask them why they want to keep the relationship a secret. You deserve much more than a secret relationship. Most times, people that propose a secret relationship just want to have a temporary thing with you while they pursue a serious relationship with someone else. Do not set yourself up for heartbreak by participating in relationships that has erroneous beginnings.

~~ Ignoring Glaring Warning Signals: Many singles ignore signs that indicate that they are heading for heartbreak. They allow emotions, desperation and pressure to blind them from seeing things in their relationships that could jeopardize their future. Some people get so emotionally entangled that they begin to look for ways to spiritualize the warning signals to sooth their selfish desires. They go as far as believing that it is God's will for them to change or convert the people displaying these warning signals. It is the Holy Spirit that convicts and converts people; trying to do this on your own will only make you frustrated and heartbroken at the end of the day. Do not carry a cross that God has not given you; it will only end up being excess luggage without benefits.

Cheating, lying, physical abuse, drug and alcohol addictions and many other vices are things you should take seriously if they are present in the life of the person you are dating or courting. Although it is vital to be helpful to people in need, when pursuing a relationship with someone as a single person, it is important they heal from such things before you make the serious commitment of walking down the aisle with them.

As a believer, God will always be faithful in showing warning signals if you are heading toward trouble. The problem is that we often ignore His voice and tend to yield to the voice of our emotions and selfish desires instead.

~~ Ignoring the Voice of the Holy Spirit: The steps of the righteous man are directed by the Lord. It is very expensive to disobey the voice of the Spirit. Some go as far as rebuking the voice of God because it is in conflict with their desires. Obeying God's voice is a sure way to avoid disaster in the future. When we follow God's direction, we will always have cause to thank Him at the end of the day.

Overcoming the Effects of a Heartbreak:

Some heartbreaks occur for unavoidable reasons. These include situations that bring a relationship to an abrupt end, including medical, incompatibility, death, parental disapproval, etc.

Whichever may be the case, if you are presently going through heartbreak for avoidable or unavoidable reasons, it is very important you know that this is not the end of your life. You might be in so much pain and think that you may never make it through. The truth is, there is light at the end of the tunnel. It may not feel like it now, but so many people have made it through with God's help. I have come across so many people who thought that they would never be able to recover from their heartbreak, but their story is different today. God has healed their pain and they can now fall in love again.

Satan will always lie to you and fill your mind with all kinds of negative things when you are going through the pain of heartbreak. He is a liar. If you choose to believe God's words concerning you, restoration is not far away from you.

It is important you know that God is interested in every aspect of your life, including your love life. Your present pain will soon be a thing of the past. The Bible says in Isaiah 43:19: "Behold, I will do a thing, now it shall spring forth; shall you not know it? I will even make a road in the wilderness and rivers in the desert." God specializes in doing the impossible. He can turn you circumstance around regardless of how grim it is at the moment. If you are yet to heal from heartbreak and you are presently experiencing its devastating effects, the following scriptures will bless you - Jeremiah 29:11-12; Joel 2:25; Isaiah 43:18.

God is faithful and just to heal your heart and restore you to a better position to love again. Get rid of bitterness, resentment and unforgiveness; surrender your heart to the Lord so He can perform a miracle in your heart.

Chapter Fifteen

Sexual Temptations:

We encounter all kinds of temptations in today's world, and the way we respond to these temptations affects both us and the people around us. Yielding to or overcoming a temptation has side effects.

Temptations are acts that look appealing. The benefits of these acts are usually short-term. Afterwards, they always lead to regrets. Temptations may appear sweet, but there are always negative consequences attached to them. Temptations can also be said to be the coaxing of a person into committing an act via curiosity, desire or manipulation.

So many Christian singles fall into sexual sin because they allow themselves to be lured by the enemy via lust, desires, ignorance and disobedience. The plan of the enemy is to make us lose fellowship with God, and one of the ways he does this is to deceive singles into defiling God's temple (their body).

While Jesus was on earth, He told His disciples to, "Watch and pray, that ye enter not into temptation: the spirit is indeed willing, but the flesh is weak" (Matthew 26:41). We need to constantly guard against temptations by watching and praying.

Jesus was Himself tempted by the devil in Matthew chapter 4. The good news is that He overcame the enemy with the Word. Since Christ was tempted, you will also face temptations in this life.

Yielding to sexual temptations has ruined many relationships, marriages, ministries, businesses and destinies. It is not a sin to be tempted; yielding to temptation is the problem. We constantly see things on the streets, in the media, at work and even in our local churches that has a sexual undertone. These sexual undertones fill our minds with all kinds of thoughts and imaginations that gradually lead people to the point where they eventually give in to a sexual trap, especially in their moment of weakness, lust or curiosity.

God is faithful and just not to leave you stranded in temptations. The Scripture says in 1st Corinthians 10:13: "No temptation has seized you except what is common to man. And God is faithful; he will not let you be tempted beyond what you can bear. But when you are tempted, he will also provide a way out so that you can stand up under it." God will always make a way out for us anytime we are faced with a temptation. Sadly, many refuse to find that way of escape and they allow their flesh to take control of the situation especially when it comes to sexual temptations.

I once read an interesting article that claimed that the number one reason for divorce was infidelity. Many people have wrecked their families and put their children through pain just because they gave in to a moment of sexual temptation.

Dealing With Sexual Temptations

You may not be able to totally control what you hear or see, but you can control the effect they have on you. The enemy goes after our minds in order to make us ponder and magnify the sexual pictures and thoughts he daily tries to insert into our minds. His ultimate aim is to create an atmosphere where he can get us to implement his suggestions.

It is important to realize that the enemy will always tempt us in line with the things we desire and lust after. He capitalizes on people's weaknesses and uses their desires against them. The book of James paints a perfect picture of the process of falling into temptation as well as the consequences of yielding to them (James 1:12).

Let us now look at ways to overcome sexual temptation:

• Flee: The most practical way of overcoming sexual temptation is to flee as recommended in 1 Corinthians 6:18. Many people face situations of sexual temptation and try to talk their way around it. When Potiphar's wife tempted Joseph, he fled the scene; he did not engage her in a long chat. If you stay longer than necessary in an environment garnished by sexual temptation, it is only a matter of time before you fall. As a single person, whenever you find yourself in a place with someone who is trying to seduce you or lure you into sexual sin, leave the place. By so doing, you will preserve yourself. Are you dating or courting someone? Do not hang out in places or with people that could make you give in to sexual immorality. The pleasure is temporal but the pain and regret that follows may last for a long time.

• Reject evil and immoral thoughts: Rejecting and preventing evil thoughts from germinating in your mind is as good as preventing a potential evil act. Whenever immoral thoughts and pictures come to your mind, reject them and begin to speak God's word over your mind. The scripture encourages us in this way: "Finally, brothers and sisters, whatever is true, whatever is noble, whatever is right, whatever is pure, whatever is lovely, whatever is admirable— if anything is excellent or praiseworthy—think about such things" (Philippians 4:8). Do not allow dirty thoughts to permeate your mind. Reject them and meditate on things that will edify you and glorify God because you will eventually carry out what you keep thinking about.

• Constant communion with the Holy Spirit: You will have little or no time for the works of the flesh if you are constantly communing with the Holy Spirit. You will be alert and respond to His promptings that will in turn deliver you from the snare of the enemy.

• Discipline and self-control: There are so many people who are not religious, yet they are able to deal with temptations by discipline and self-control. Build a habit of saying "no" to any form of premarital sex and sexual temptations. However, there is a limit to which discipline and self-control can take you; rely more on the Holy Spirit who always gives the believer an edge in maintaining a life of discipline and self-control.

How you respond to the sexual temptations you encounter today can determine the kind of future you create for yourself and future generations. Honour God in and with your body; allow Him to saturate your mind and victory will be yours in the days of temptation.

If you have fallen several times into sexual temptation, God's love can reach you and restore you. He can make your life whole again. Do not remain on the floor; you can rise again. God is able and willing to forgive you if only you will let Him take over your life. You cannot overcome sexual sins on your own. You need the divine help of the Holy Spirit to quicken you and give you wisdom and power over sexual sins.

Chapter Sixteen

Soul Ties:

This is a very sensitive subject many singles are ignorant of. A lot of people suffer from the effects of soul ties for years and decades of their lives. It is possible to suffer from the effects of a soul tie from a previous relationship even after one is long married.

Before we examine "soul ties", let us look at what a "soul" is.

The human soul is one of the three components of every human being. Every human being is a spirit who possesses a soul and lives in a body. Our spirit is the aspect of us that is eternal and our soul is the side of us that consists of our mind, will and emotion. Our body on the other hand is the part of man that is visible to us physically; it is the container and frame we use to operate on this earthly realm. There is more to life than the things we see with our naked eye, as a matter of fact the realities of the invisible world are much more than the realities of the visible world. You can get more information on the three major aspects of humans in my previous book "True Fulfillment."

As mentioned above, our soul is the aspect of us that is made up of the mind, will and emotions. With our minds we think and imagine things; with our will we are able to make decisions and with our emotions we are able to reflect our mood, temperament and personality disposition. The soul is so important, and we need to be careful what and who we allow to influence it.

As Christians our soul is the most sought after target by the devil. He tries all he can to gain control of it whenever we let him. The activities of your soul on this earth realm will ultimately determine your eternal destination when you exit this world. No wonder the scripture say in Mark 8:36: "For what shall it profit a man, if he gains the whole world and lose his own soul?"

Knowing how vital your soul is will make you more conscious of your activities in this life.

Let us now look into what a soul tie is. The term "**soul tie**" refers to the interdependence, linkage or knitting of the soul of two or more people to the point where they influence the mind, will and emotions of each other. Many people may be conscious or unconscious of this kind of influence someone may have over them.

Many people have wrecked their courtships, marriages and lives as a result of the effect of a negative soul tie that they have with someone else. There are healthy and unhealthy soul ties. A soul tie can be a good thing if it is between you and someone you are married to.

Lets us take a look at some situations where a healthy soul tie exists:

In the book of Genesis 2:24 the Bible says, "Therefore shall a man leave his father and his mother, and cleave to his wife: and they shall be one flesh." This scripture is the perfect illustration of a positive soul tie. The term "one flesh" has been misinterpreted by so many people over the years. What the scripture means here is that, when a man completely leaves his father and mother and cleaves to his wife who also has completely left her father and mother then, they shall become one flesh. In other words, they become good soul mates.

Obviously, oneness here is not physical (bodily) oneness as this is not possible. When people get married, they do not disappear and become a single being. The oneness there is also not referring to oneness in spirit, because that is not possible either. Your spirit is an eternal identity that is unique to you alone. We can only work with other people to achieve a unified spiritual purpose, but we can never be one in spirit literarily with them. The only person we can be one with in spirit is God (I Corinthians 6:17), because we originate from Him.

The oneness in flesh between married people is in the knitting of their souls. They become so knitted that they become like-minded. This like-mindedness makes them work and walk together in harmony. Unfortunately, only a few married couples enjoy this great power of being knitted in their soul. This knitting is not forced; it happens willingly and naturally because it is driven by pure love. It does not imply that parties to a marriage will lose their uniqueness or their identity; it only means that they have chosen to come together and unify themselves strongly in order to enjoy and make the most of their relationship.

This explains why you see some married couples who think and act alike to the point where one of them can make a decision for the other without a fight because they know each other so well. They are not just connected in the body, but also in their soul. Knowing your spouse or future spouse beyond the physical realm will give you a strong edge in building a strong relationship. It goes beyond sexual chemistry and connection.

Another situation where a healthy soul tie may exist is in a strong natural friendship. This friendship is not romantic or sexual in nature; it is purely based on understanding and a deep connection in the soul. Some people have this connection with people they call "best mates".

A good example of this is the relationship that existed between Jonathan and David in the scriptures. They were so connected that Jonathan ultimately put his life and the throne of his father on the line in order to protect his friendship with David. The Bible recorded in 1 Samuel 18:1: "And it came to pass when he had made an end of speaking to Saul, that the soul of Jonathan was knit with the soul of David."

Some friends enjoy this strong bond between them so much that they go to great lengths to be there for their friends and protect their friendships without any sexual or selfish strings attached. This strong bond may also exist between members of the same family. It is a very strong connection that makes you understand and be there for each other without expecting anything in return.

Unhealthy soul ties on the other hand have trapped many single people to the point where they are unable to enjoy their present relationships. They are unable to move forward in life because they are still tied to someone they met in the past. This could be more devastating when married couples, who though married, are unable to enjoy their spouses because they are tied to someone else in their past in the soul realm.

I have come across and counselled so many married people whose problems were traceable to one or both parties being soul-tied to someone from their previous relationship. Marriages reeling under the effect of a soul tie will often break down for no visible reason.

I met a lady recently who is married to a good man who loves and provides for her. But she could not tell the reason why she is never happy with him. During counselling, I discovered that she was still tied in the soul with her ex-boyfriend. Though her relationship with her ex-boyfriend ended 17 years before she met her husband, and there was no contact between them whatsoever, she was still knitted with the guy in her soul. Unconsciously, she was constantly comparing the ex with her present husband. This comparison made her not able to see her husband for who he really was. She could not celebrate her husband's strengths because she was constantly comparing him with another person from her past. After prayers and counselling, she is now enjoying her marriage. Comparing your spouse or the person you are in a relationship with to someone else is a sure way to blind yourself from seeing and appreciating them for who they really are.

So many singles have tied themselves in the soul realm with people who have negatively influenced their lives in the past. I have seen so many singles trapped in addictions, spiritual oppression, depression and abuse of all types because they involved themselves in relationships with some people who left a negative effect in their lives. When we go into relationships with people of the opposite sex, we become very vulnerable because of the love and feeling we have for them. However, there are some practices and things some singles engage in that can become avenues for people to negatively influence them and make them tied in the soul even long after the relationship ends. Some of these things are as follows:

Premarital Sex: For every sexual intercourse encounter a single person engages in, he or she creates an avenue for a soul tie. Sexual intercourse is not just a physical activity; it is much more than that. Like I have said before, anytime you have sex with someone, a part of you is left in that person and a part of that person is left in you. This is why you still think about them strongly even if they are not present. A lot of invisible activities take place during sexual intercourse. Demonic spirits are transferred during illegitimate intercourse. This is why so many people who are seemingly

OK suddenly begin to experience setbacks, demonic oppression, depression and hallucinations because they had sex with somebody with spiritual complications.

Save sex for marriage, apart from the obvious sexually transmitted diseases, there are spiritually transmitted diseases infecting many singles on a daily basis because of premarital sexual relations with people influenced by evil spirits. One Corinthians 6:16 paints a good picture of what we are talking about. It says, "Or do you not know that he who is joined to a harlot is one body with her? For the two He says 'shall become one flesh.'"

The word "harlot' in this scripture is not just referring to a prostitute (male or female); it also refers to anyone or anything that tries to defile God's temple (your body). Do not carry or burden yourself with spiritual baggage or hindrance because of premarital sex. Keep your body whole and wait on God's timing with the right person.

Unhealthy Infatuation: Someone can be said to be suffering from infatuation when he or she kicks "reasoning" out and becomes engulfed by an addictive passion or admiration towards another person. This feeling is usually short-lived and it can be very destructive to the person who is caged in the state of infatuation. Many people mistake infatuation for love. The truth is, they are certainly not the same. You can be in love with someone and be caught up in infatuation, but not every case of infatuation emanates from love.

So many singles find themselves in relationships where they display dangerous infatuation towards the person they are in a relationship with to the point where they end up getting shattered. Some singles however, become infatuated with people they are not even in a relationship with; they admire someone so strongly that they begin to think about them day and night. Their mind becomes full of thoughts most of which are unhealthy and foul. Some of these

143

unhealthy thoughts have led some to do things they later regretted.

Infatuation can lead to a soul tie. The person who is infatuated can become trapped by his or her thoughts, thus giving the devil a platform to build a stronghold over their minds. They can become unconsciously tied to the person they are infatuated by, long after the person physically leaves the scene of their lives. Afterwards, they become unable to give someone else a chance to love them.

\# Low Self-Esteem: There are so many people suffering from low self-esteem. They constantly need validation from the people around them to keep their head above the waters of life.

Some singles with very low self-esteem only feel better when they are beside the person they are in a relationship with. They feel crippled and stagnant when the person is not around them. They can hardly function effectively without the person they are in a relationship with by their side. They become so attached to their lover to the point where an unhealthy soul-tie is formed between them. So much so that they can become suicidal or depressed if the person decides to end the relationship.

Unhealthy soul ties often lead to demonic oppression, emotional instability and even marital disharmony. If you are currently suffering from the effects of an unhealthy soul tie, your situation is not hopeless; God can deliver you and set you free. If only you come to Him, He is able and willing to step into your situation and turn it around.

I met a young man from West Africa sometime back who was suffering from the effects of a negative soul tie. He was caged by the influence his ex-girlfriend had on him. He could not move on even though the ex-girlfriend was long married to someone else. He kept staggering anytime he met someone he wanted to build a relationship with. He would mention her name in his sleep; he would unconsciously compare the people he dated with her. The enemy successfully built a stronghold over his mind. He was so miserable until he encountered God, and after prayer and counselling, the yoke was broken and he was able to find true love in a lovely lady who is now his wife. There is nothing God cannot do! He can break the chains over your soul and make you whole again.

Chapter Seventeen

Forgiveness:

Forgiveness is a companion everyone in a relationship needs to carry along in the journey of life. Matters of the heart are very sensitive.

In life, we may consciously or unconsciously hurt the people around us and they may also hurt us too. The people we are in a relationship with will at one point or another hurt us through their actions or words, and we need to learn how to let go and forgive them when they offend us.

So many Christian singles are heartbroken and offended by people who have hurt them in one way or the other at various stages in their lives, and as a result of this they carry the hurt everywhere they go. You might have been lied to, cheated and betrayed by someone you trusted and loved, and are now harbouring unforgiveness towards them. You need to forgive.

As believers, it is very important we get to the point where we let go and forgive the people that offend us. If God can forgive us our sins, then we need to forgive the people who offend us as well. God expects us to forgive, because lack of forgiveness hinders us from receiving God's forgiveness; it also affects us directly in many other ways. In the long run it is the person that refuses to forgive that loses the most.

Unforgiveness can hinder you spiritually and medically. I read a medical article the other day that said that unforgiveness can increase people's chances of having high blood pressure, heart disease, cancer, stroke, weak immune system, etc. Unforgiveness can shorten your lifespan. It is not worth it, so let it go! Unforgiveness destroys you and the people around you; it steals your joy.

Forgiving people that deliberately hurt you can be very painful at first, but at the end of the day, the benefits of forgiveness are better than the price of unforgiveness. On your own you cannot forgive the people that hurt you; you need the help of the Holy Spirit. Forgiveness takes away burdens from you and sets you free to have an unhindered relationship with God. Forgiving people with the help of the Holy Spirit goes beyond human comprehension. Man's wisdom is framed on revenge and retaliation, but the best avenger is God. Leave the issues in His hands.

When we operate in the power of forgiveness, we may appear foolish to the people around us, but the power it releases is unquantifiable. Operating in forgiveness releases you from limitations; it makes you healthier; it makes your prayers go to God unhindered.

The benefits of operating in forgiveness are countless You are able to hear from God smoothly when you forgive the people that offend you. Are you hurting? Has someone broken your heart? Did someone betray you? Ask the Holy Spirit to help you forgive and as you do so, the Lord will begin to heal your heart and life, beyond your widest imaginations.

I met a lady several years ago who was subjected to a lot of pain by her ex-boyfriend. He cheated on her repeatedly and left her for another lady shortly before they were to get married. She was full of bitterness and as a result of these painful experiences, she was unforgiving towards her ex. She finally decided to forgive and let go of the hurt with the help of the Holy Spirit. It was hard for her at first, but she did it.

About a year later, I saw her and she looked totally different. She looked healthier, happier and full of life. The transformation was from the inside out. God restored her and even blessed her with a decent relationship. All this happened only after she decided to truly let go.

Lack of forgiveness hinders a brighter future from unfolding before you; it delays you in the journey of life. Regardless of what you have been through, it is all in the past, and your future is more important than your past.

Let go and let God!

Chapter Eighteen

When to Say Goodbye:

M illions of singles across the globe are trapped in toxic relationships. These relationships trap them and hinder them from fulfilling their God-given purposes in life. Many are unable to pursue their career, education, hobbies and dreams in life because they are consumed by the many distractions and depletion that comes with being in noxious relationships. A good number of people know they are in relationships that do them no good, but they keep holding on for various reasons.

Saying goodbye to a relationship may be very difficult, especially when your heart is fully committed to it and you have invested your precious time into it. Many single people in toxic relationships fail to understand that a broken relationship is better than a broken life. Holding on to a toxic relationship will eventually do damage to you in many ways. Although most relationships go through rough patches and time is needed for them to even out, some relationships are toxic and dangerous; they need to be brought to a quick end in order to save one or both parties from ruining their lives.

I have seen so many single people who do well in their career, faith and life, only to put all these at risk by involving themselves in toxic relationships. The health and state of your relationship goes a long way to positively or negatively affect other areas of your life. This is why it is very important to be vigilant and not get trapped in toxic relationships.

Until you learn to summon the courage to "say goodbye" to a poisonous relationship, you may eventually find yourself moving in reverse in the journey of life. Refusing or not having the courage to say goodbye to a bad relationship can make you believe that such relationships are the norm.

God is always eager and ready to take us to the next level in our walk with Him and in the fulfilment of our purposes, but we are hindered many times by the people we form alliances with. So many singles remain and hold on to destructive relationships because of the lies the enemy has told them, lies that make them feel they do not deserve the best. The enemy sometimes tells them they are ugly, fat and undeserving. The devil is a liar! The truth is: until you get rid of a toxic relationship, you may not encounter a healthy relationship.

Father Abraham in the book of Genesis never got the child of promise (Isaac) until he sent Ishmael away. God is willing and waiting to reveal the right relationship to you, but you need to get rid of the toxic people and relationships in your life in order to pave the way for the perfect will of God.

In Genesis 13, Abraham had to separate himself from Lot when the relationship between their herdsmen became toxic. The very moment Abraham parted from Lot, God spoke to him and revealed the extent to which he was going to posses the land. We need to end our companionship and relationship with people who distract us and take us out of God's plan for our lives. This will help us to hear from God clearly and move to the next level in life. Holding on to toxic people in our lives will delay us on the journey of life.

Do not allow sentiment, tradition, fear, friends and people's opinion to deter you from separating yourself from toxic relationships. Below are some circumstances that constitute a toxic relationship. If as a single person you find yourself in these circumstances, you are advised to call it quit and say goodbye for your own good and for the good of your future generation.

> Physical Abuse: Do not accept physical abuse to be a norm in a relationship. If a man or a woman constantly abuses you as a single person, they will most likely do the same when they get married to you. We cherish, love and adore the people we genuinely love; we do not become violent towards them. In the United Kingdom, the office of statistics says that one in four women will be victims of domestic violence. Domestic violence is on the rise and you should not stay put in a relationship with someone that is violent towards you. Say goodbye. Speak out and seek help. Both men and women can be victims of physical abuse, but whatever your gender may be, if you find yourself in an abusive relationship, you are advised to say goodbye.

> Seeing a Married Man or Woman: It a shameful thing for a married person to have an extra-marital affair and it is equally shameful for a single person to go into a relationship with a married person. It constitutes a toxic relationship worthy of saying "goodbye" to.

No matter the promises a married person makes to you as a single person, you should simply say "no". Whatever we sow in life, we will eventually reap. I have seen so many single sisters who secretly or openly dated married men and caused deep pain for the wives. Most of these single sisters eventually experience the same thing themselves when they got married. Beware of what you sow. Wait patiently on God for you own man or woman. Do not take someone else's wife or husband. It is a toxic relationship. If you find yourself in such a situation, regardless of the benefits, it is time to say "goodbye" and ask God for forgiveness.

➤ Absence of Love: What is the point of being in a relationship that is void of love? Love should be the basis upon which a relationship is built. Unfortunately, many have traded love for sex, wealth and other self-gratifying things that cannot compare with love. No matter the gravity of love you have for someone, if they do not love you in return, you are going to struggle a great deal. A relationship becomes sweeter when parties to it mutually love each other. If as a single person you find yourself in a relationship where you are told that you are no longer loved, wisdom demands that you say goodbye because, without love, there is nothing to build upon.

➤ Heading Nowhere: It is very important not to waste your time and life in a relationship that is not heading anywhere. So many people involve themselves in relationships that have no defined destination. They remain in such relationships for baseless reasons. A life without purpose is a life that is being wasted. Do not get stuck with people who tell you the same old stories year after year without having any direction whatsoever for their relationship with you.

A man told me how he was in a relationship with a girl that spanned almost a decade without knowing where they were heading. Anytime he talked about marriage, she would be evasive and put him on hold. On the other hand, anytime he wanted to move on with his life, she would ask for more time. He eventually summoned the courage to say "goodbye" after wasting almost ten years. It is very important you define your relationships. Have objectives, goals and a purpose for the relationship. Everything may not happen as planned, but defining your relationship goes a long way toward painting a picture of where you are heading. Wake up and say "goodbye" to any undefined relationship that is taking you nowhere.

➤ Unequally Yoked: Many Christian singles expect God to bless what He does not endorse. God will not contradict His words. The scripture clearly tell us not to be unequally yoked with unbelievers. This statement is so true, especially in the area of relationships and marriage. Are you single and are you currently in a relationship that does not glorify God? You can say goodbye. Relationships are meant to build and nourish you spiritually, which is why being in a relationship with someone who is not compatible with you spiritually can be a big problem along the way. Summon the courage to say "goodbye" if you are in such a relationship. It is spiritually toxic.

➤ A Perpetual Cheat or Liar: People who consistently and unrepentantly cheat on you before marriage are likely to do the same thing even in marriage. Although I believe in the power of forgiveness, but when the signs become too glaring, it may be time to say "goodbye" and avoid future pain and heartbreak. It is a sign of total disrespect to cheat on someone you are in a relationship with, whether married or not. Sometimes, as a single person, in addition to forgiving someone for cheating on or lying to you, you should also tell them goodbye for a season or for life.

➤ When the Holy Spirit Says So: The Holy Spirit is the most reliable adviser in a relationship and no matter how picture-perfect a relationship may look on the surface, if the Holy Spirit tells you to exit it, you need to obey Him and say goodbye to the relationship. We serve a God that sees the very end from the very beginning; He knows all things. Hearken, therefore, to His voice anytime He speaks to you.

Abraham A Jones

Section 6

Chapter Nineteen
Reality

So many single men and women have their minds full of ideas and imaginations on how their life would be after they get married to the wife or husband of their dreams. Hollywood has given so many people the wrong impression of marital life. Movies have a way of creating a picture of "happily-ever-after" marriages and as a result, a lot of singles become confused when they get married and see the opposite of what they always dreamed of. It is very easy to put on a fairy tale proposal or a fairy tale wedding ceremony if you have they money; but there is no amount of money that can give you a fairy tale marriage. No successful marriage is void of one challenge or another.

What makes a marriage successful is not the absence of challenges, but the ability of couples to stick together even in spite of them. The fairy tale mentality many people have about marriage has led to the early collapse of so many marriages. After all, celebrity marriages break down despite the millions of dollars spent to organize a fairy tale proposal and a fairy tale wedding.

It is worth repeating that marriage begins after the wedding. The wedding is an event that lasts for a few hours, but marriage is meant to be for life. Marriage is another phase of learning and knowing more about the person you are married to. Whilst married, you will discover many things about your spouse's attitude, habits, strengths and weaknesses. Some of your discoveries will be pleasant and some of them may not be.

A lady dated and courted a guy for several years and never knew that he snored. A few days into their marriage, she became so frustrated by the vibrating sound of her husband's snoring. She never saw that aspect of him while they were dating. It came as a surprise to her that her husband who always looked and smelt good could be someone who also snored!

We live in a generation where we are so eager to throw things away just because they are broken. However, not every broken thing should be thrown away. Marriages go through difficult times, but this does not mean you should exit the marriage. Before you get married, you need to understand the fact that marriage is not a fairy tale; it is a true experience that involves real people. No matter how hard you try to pretend when dating or courting somebody, it will be a different ball game when you get married. Your true identity will emerge over time. This is why it is very important to work on yourself before you step into the territory of marriage. It is better you get there late and prepared to succeed than for you to rush in with a mind full of deceptive myths.

Don't get me wrong; marriage is a beautiful thing especially when you marry someone that you love and who also loves you in return. However, even in a loving relationship, challenges may arise to challenge the love that exists between couples. I always tell single people that one of the ways to meet the right person is to be the right person yourself. Instead of waiting to meet the perfect man or the perfect woman, invest in yourself and develop yourself to become someone worth calling Mister or Miss right.

Do not give up on a God-given relationship just because you are faced with a challenge. If you refuse to give up, the challenge will make you stronger and reinforce the bond of love between you and your spouse.

Revelation Versus Manifestation

God is very good at revealing things to His children. He does not keep His children in the dark. A lot of us have dreams, visions and revelations about our future, relationships and life in general. Many believers receive prophecies and promises from various ministers of the gospel and directly from the Lord through His word or His Spirit. Nothing takes God by surprise because He is all knowing and all powerful.

Nonetheless, it is one thing for you to receive a revelation, and another thing for you to see it manifest on the earthly realm. When God gives us a promise or a revelation about the things that He is going to do in our lives, those things automatically come into existence in the spirit realm. The entire universe was created from the words that came out of His mouth. Anytime God gives us a promise, the manifestation of such a promise is already in existence in the invisible realm. The problem is that not everybody that receives a promise or prophecy sees the physical manifestation of such a prophetic word or promise. Many believers become confused when the circumstances around them are contrary to what was spoken to them by the Lord. As a result, they allow the enemy to sow seeds of doubt and unbelief in their hearts.

Sometimes, the earthly timeline between a prophecy and the manifestation the prophecy can be discouraging if we focus solely on the things that our naked eyes can see. Just because there is a delay in the manifestation of a prophetic word in your life does not mean that it will not come to pass.

Many people give up in their walk with God because the enemy lied to them and discouraged them along the way.

Whenever I read the scriptures and look at the lives of great men and women like Abraham, Sarah, Joseph and David, I imagine how they could wait for decades to see the manifestation of God's purpose for their lives. If they had given up along the way they wouldn't have been able to see the manifestation of God's promises. Many marriages and relationships have crashed not because they were not the will of God, but because one or both parties in the relationship or marriage could not hold on to the promise until the manifestation stage. The enemy will always fight anyone who is on a mission from the Lord.

Some of the greatest weapons the enemy uses to dislodge God's children these days are fear, doubt and unbelief. He sows these seeds in the heart of believers so he can abort God's prophetic word that is about to be made manifest in their lives.

Has God revealed anything to you concerning your life? Has He showed you a vision about you future, home, career or marriage? Stand firm and hold to it until you see the full manifestation of the prophecy. God is not a man that He should lie. Whatever He says, He will do. Even when there seems to be a wide gap between the revelation and its manifestation, with the eyes of faith, you will be able to see things as God sees them. Look, therefore, into the realms of the spirit and speak the manifestation of such revelation into existence. Regardless of what you see around you physically, refuse to doubt God's word and stand firm upon His promises. Do not give up on your relationship, marriage and calling just because you cannot yet see the manifestation of what was revealed to you. God is about to make them manifest in and around you for all to see and to glorify His name. You are closer to your promised land now than you have ever been before. Do not give in and do not give up; God is about to put a lasting smile on your face.

Spiritual Warfare

Many people shy away from spiritual warfare in their relationships and marriages. The devil is very much interested in destroying relationships and families. He understands that whoever influences the home, will eventually control society. The things we see physically here in the earthly realm are just a reflection of the things occurring in the spirit realm.

Many people have lost out on decent relationships and marriages because they lacked understanding regarding spiritual warfare. The devil thrives in an environment saturated by ignorance. Do not get caught off guard. Do not be deceived either. There is a battle going on and your relationship is very much part of this war. Satan seeks to ruin God-ordained relationships and distract couples from God's will and purpose for their lives. As believers, we are soldiers on the battlefield and our common enemy is the devil. It will be a great tragedy to be negligent or careless while this war is on.

There are two major forces patrolling and controlling the earth today and like it or not, our lives and relationships are controlled and influenced by one of these forces. These are the forces of good (God) and evil (Satan). These two forces are not on the same path and they are constantly at war with each other.

You need to learn how to fight and rebuke the enemy of your relationship when he comes around. So many people use physical means to fight the devil when he comes knocking at their door. They become frustrated in the process because you cannot use physical techniques to fight a spiritual enemy. When you see the traces of the works of the enemy in and around your relationship or in the life of the person you are in a relationship with, cursing, swearing, nagging or even fighting will only make matters worse. There is a spirit behind every action and intelligent Christians fight spiritual battles effectively by addressing the spirit behind the actions; they refrain from fighting the man or woman that is influenced by an evil spirit to act in a certain way. There are spirits behind actions like lying, alcohol addiction, drug addiction, pornography, sexual immorality, etc. We get better results when we deal with the spirits behind these acts before we even start addressing the issues physically.

I have seen many relationships that came under severe attack from the pits of hell be healed and restored because one or both parties in the relationships knew what to do spiritually. Instead of fighting in the flesh, they stood their ground in the Lord and resisted the devil by speaking God's word into their circumstance in the place of prayer. Over time, God came through for them.

Do not be ignorant of the devices of the evil one. Invest quality time in the place of prayer over your relationships. Many singles wait until they are married before they begin to engage in spiritual warfare for their future family. Pray in advance and commit your future spouse, children and entire family into God's hands. It is often said that the best form of defence is "attack". Do not wait for things to go wrong before you arm yourself in prayer. Be on guard and initiate spiritual programs between you and the person you are in a relationship with in order to build spiritual stamina to fight in the days of battle.

In Ephesians 6:12, the scriptures make us to understand that we do not wrestle against flesh and blood, but we are fighting against spiritual forces. Behind every physical adversary is a spirit that influences words and actions. Dealing with the physical adversary alone, therefore, is futile and unproductive. Jesus looked at his disciple, Peter, and said, "Get thee behind me Satan" (Matthew 16:23).

Instead of rebuking Peter, Jesus addressed the spirit that propelled Peter to speak and act the way he did. When the enemy captures the heart, words and actions of the people in our lives, it is important we address the spirit behind their actions in the place of prayer.

The good news is that we are on the winning side of this battle. Jesus said in John 16:33 that we should be of good cheer because He has overcome the world. The devil is no match for the power of our God. Engage in warfare, therefore, with the mentality of a victor. Fight from the standpoint of victory that was given to us by the finished work of the cross. Refuse to be a victim by arming yourself with the whole amour of God. Confidently rebuke the enemy from the life of your loved ones when he comes knocking at the door and he will flee from you. There is power in the word of God and in the name of Jesus.

Chapter Twenty

The Role of the Holy Spirit In Relationships

Any marriage or home void of the presence of the Holy Spirit is like a ship without a compass. The Holy Spirit is more than just a cliché; He is real. He is our present-help in the time of need. The role of the Holy Spirit in our relationships and lives should not be taken for granted. He can deliver, preserve and protect us from so many dangers and disasters on the journey of life.

Jesus promised us the Holy Spirit before His ascension because He knew that we could not successfully navigate our way here on earth without the direction and leading of the Holy Spirit. No wonder the scriptures say in Romans 8:14: "As many that are led by the Spirit of God, they are the sons of God."

Reading through the scriptures you will discover an array of functions of the Holy Spirit in our lives. He is our comforter, teacher, helper, revealer of truth, reminder, etc. Life is dry and empty without the Holy Spirit. The Greek word "Pneuma" used for the Holy Spirit in the New Testament, means to "breathe". A relationship without the leading, promptings and convictions of the Holy Spirit is as good as dead. As the comforter, the Holy Spirit comforts you deep within where no man or woman can reach. He comforts us in ways that no one can ever do. As a teacher, the Spirit teaches us things we need to know about life and relationships, and as the revealer of truth the Holy Spirit can reveal hidden things to you, things that ordinarily would never have come to light.

The Holy Spirit gives us divine direction and empowerment in various aspects of our lives. You cannot afford not to have Him in your relationship and life. He makes your life and relationship a lot easier and sweeter.

One of the things the Holy Spirit helps us with in our relationships is the ability to produce the fruit of the Spirit. This is a necessary development in the life of every believer who wants to enjoy his or her relationship, marriage and home.

In Galatians 5:22-23, we were shown nine fruit of the Spirit. You cannot bear this fruit without the help of the Holy Spirit. Trying to produce love, joy, peace, longsuffering, gentleness, goodness, faith, meekness and temperance on your own is impossible. Many relationships and marriages failed because of the absence of the fruit of the Spirit in the lives of the couples. Believers who allow the Holy Spirit to work this fruit in and through them will no doubt have successful, long-lasting and fulfilling relationships.

The best time to produce the fruit of the spirit is while you are still single. It makes you radiate God's life and it distinguishes you from people who do not have the fruit. Stop trying to be a good man or woman all by yourself; get the Holy Spirit involved and you will begin to reflect the kingdom life with little or no struggle. For with God, all things are possible.

The Power of Appreciation

Appreciation is a virtue many people neglect in our generation. We take many things for granted because we do not value and appreciate them the way we ought to. Failure to appreciate some things in life will eventually make the value of those things depreciate in our eyes. God placed people in our lives so we can appreciate them, and the more we appreciate them, the more they feel valued and loved. A person who feels appreciated will go the extra mile for those who show such gratitude.

Appreciation is very significant. God Himself appreciated the work of His hands during creation in Genesis 1:25. Many people take their spouses, fiancés and fiancées for granted only to end up losing them. It is after losing them that they realize how important they were in their lives. Do not wait until you forfeit your God-given relationships before you learn to place value on them.

It is sad to see people die without being appreciated by the people in their lives. Expensive tombstones, coffins or flowers for their graves cannot be compared to showing them love while they are alive. Do not wait until the people in your life pass away before you acknowledge and appreciate them. Let them know that you care while they are alive. Tell and show them how you feel about them. Do not wait until you can appreciate them in a big way before you express your gratitude to them. Little things like compliments, flowers, cards, notes, encouragements, scriptures and prayers will go a long way to make somebody feel loved and appreciated.

When we appreciate the people in our lives, they are inspired to go the extra mile for us. Failure to appreciate the man, woman and people God has placed in your life may make them feel unappreciated, used and abused.

Since nobody is perfect, ignore the minor shortcomings of the person you love and celebrate their strengths. Learn to discover and explore the strengths of the person you are in a relationship with.

Appreciating your spouse has a lot of benefits. When people are appreciated, their confidence level increases, the bond of love becomes stronger, they feel valued, their faithfulness is boosted, and they willingly go to great lengths for the relationship. On the other hand, a lack of appreciation leads to a weakened love bond, lack of trust and a feeling of being used.

Just because people do things without complaining does not mean that we should not appreciate them. When we appreciate the people in our lives, it is a sign that we value them and appreciate God for sending them into out lives. Do not wait until you lose them before you know their worth. The best time to show them how much you love and care for them is now.

Ten Things You Should Never Say or Do to Someone You Love

It is very important to be conscious of the things we say and do to the people we love. When we treat the people we love the way we want them to treat us, life becomes easy because we would be very mindful and selective of what we do and say to them. Our words are very powerful. They either project life or inject death into the people we speak to. The people we love need to hear words of life that will inspire them to be better people and not toxic words that cripple them on the journey of life.

Here are some of the things you should avoid saying or doing to the person you love:

Things you should never say:

\# "I regret ever meeting you"

\# "My Ex is better than you"

\# "You are a failure"

\# "Your mates are doing better than you"

\# "You are a mistake"

Things you should not do:

\# Use what they told you in confidence against them at a later date

\# Cheat on them

\# Lie to them

\# Put them down in public

\# Abuse them

Although some people say things they do not really mean, especially when they are angry, it is crucial we make a deliberate effort to censor the words we use when speaking to the people in our lives as it can go a very long way to determine the health of your relationship with them.

Chapter Twenty-One
Intrinsic Singleness

As we conclude these discussions about singleness, I want us to take a look at the second type of singleness as stated in the first chapter: Intrinsic Singleness. We considered the first type, Relational Singleness, in chapter one, and will now touch on intrinsic singleness.

Intrinsic singleness is the type of singleness that is inherent in all of us. We were born with it and designed to live with it for the rest of our lives. Simply put, it is the DNA of your purpose; this should not be neglected or abandoned even when we get married. A good marriage will help you to fulfil your purpose in life. It does not override your purpose as many would assume. Intrinsic singleness is your identity. It is single because there can only be similarities in identities and purposes, but there can never be two purposes that are the same kind. Intrinsic singleness is what makes you unique. You do not have a duplicate. We are all designed to play unique roles in this life. Failure to play your role will leave a dark hole inside of you. You may change your name, address and status when you marry, but you do not lose your purpose and identity. Some things may change about you, but your purpose should remain and blossom.

Many people give up on what they love doing best just because they got married. As a result, they have lost their joy and sense of purpose. If you bury your purpose on account of wanting to get married, you may end up becoming unhappy later; and all it takes for a marriage or a relationship to go sour is for one party to be unfulfilled or unhappy.

Your purpose is like a seed that you have to nurture in order for it to grow and blossom. Unfortunately many abandon their "seed" and have not given it a chance to grow. Whatever the nature of your purpose and calling, you can fulfil it. Sometimes we are weighed down by people and circumstances that constantly tell us we cannot do what God called us to do and become who He created us to be. However, all things are possible for those who believe.

A wise thing to do before you get married is to discuss with the person you are in a relationship with about your passions, dreams, goals, purpose and calling in life. By so doing, you will be able to see how you can synergize your purposes together without burying them.

Priority

We live in a season that is crucial to destiny and significant in eternity. For this reason, every day, hour, minute and second COUNTS! The strategy of the evil one against believers is to make them major on the MINORS and minor on the MAJORS of life. He knows that one of your greatest assets is your TIME. If he can get you to waste or misuse it, he has robbed you both in this life and in the life to come.

You need to learn how to prioritize the activities in your life. A failure to prioritize rightly may leave you confused on the journey of life.

Below are things that should be major priorities in your life:

⋆ Priority 1 (GOD)

Do not put ANYTHING or ANYONE before God. Putting anything before God is one of the greatest misplacements of priorities of all time. How can you survive, excel or overcome without your Source? The totality of your existence is summed up in Him. Nothing and no one should take the place of God in your life.

⋆ Priority 2 (Your Purpose)

We were all designed to fulfil a purpose and carry out an assignment in life. Do not allow anything or anyone to rob you of your purpose because your earthly relevance and eternal significance depend on it. Men, women and friends will sometimes come and go, but you cannot afford to lose your purpose.

Many lives depend on the discovery and exploration of your purpose; do not let them down!

Are you going to give excuses and watch destinies that are tied to your purpose vaporize? Do not halt your purpose because of someone, a circumstance or a challenge. Press on against all odds!

NOTE: You are not an accidental product; rather you are a product of a divine calculation. There is a unique space for you, and ONLY you can fill that space.

⋆ Priority 3 (Your Time)

Although God transcends time and eternity, for every purpose there is a set time. Urgency, accuracy and promptness are crucial when walking with God and for effectiveness in life.

It is not enough to fulfil purpose; you need to fulfil it in good time. There are destinies and lives linked to every purpose. Therefore, delaying exploration of your purpose has side effects. It can trigger a negative chain reaction on both you and people you don't even know.

People who have no regard for your time, indirectly have no regard for your life. No matter how spiritual or intelligent you are, time reflects in everything you do. Just because you are aware of the grace, mercy and second-chance doctrines, does not mean you should take time for granted. The impact you make when you act in the perfect/original timing will be a lot more than the impact in any other instance. Please, make the most of your time while you still have it.

★ Priority 4 (Life)

There is a huge difference between surviving, existing and living. L.I.F.E. = Living In Fulfilment Eternally. When you know GOD, your PURPOSE and the value of TIME, living your life will be more meaningful. Living a good life is not necessarily a function of wealth and riches; it is being happy even in the face of challenges because you are persuaded that you are on the right path. You need to be in the right frame of life (spirit, soul and body) in order to fulfil purpose.

No matter how great, influential or capable you are, if you neglect the development of your mind and spirit, as well as the nurturing of your body (health), your life may be cut short. Ensure you are healthy in every area of your life. Failure to do this may hinder you from living a good life regardless of your knowledge of God, purpose or the value you place on time.

It is worth repeating that there is more to life than marriage. When all is said and done and you finally exit this world, God is not going to reward you based on whether you were married or not; He is going to reward you based on how much of His will you accomplished.

Seek and fulfil your purpose in God. You will enjoy your relationship or marriage more when your spouse or the person you are in a relationship with finds you fulfilling your God-given purpose. May the eyes of your understanding be enlightened and may you discover your purpose and fulfil it to the fullest.

The Book

You don't need to be in a relationship in order to be complete and you don't need a man or a woman in your life in order to feel complete as a person. God didn't create you as an incomplete person; He created you complete from the very beginning.

Many people are failing in their relationships, marriages and lives as a result of a lack of understanding of who they are, what singleness is all about, and the purpose of relationships. This book unveils life-transforming and doubt-dissolving truths on how to understand and enjoy singleness. It gives vital information that will equip and prepare you for a serious relationship or marriage.

Many single people struggle with issues that hinder them from enjoying their singleness. They fail to understand that singleness is a phase of life that is meant to be explored and enjoyed. Rushing into a relationship or marriage in order to escape singleness has ruined many lives.

God intends for us to enjoy our single life as much as He wants us to enjoy married life. If you are not single and happy, marriage will not guarantee happiness. A happy, fulfilled and equipped single person is more likely to succeed in building a healthy relationship than a single person who is not equipped with an understanding of the purpose of singleness. Relationships are better and healthier when parties to it are intrinsically complete and happy with their singleness beforehand. This book will educate you and equip you with tools that will help you before and during your relationship.

Single & Complete is a total package that will show you the purpose of singleness, how to enjoy it, as well as prepare you with necessary truths about marriage as God intended from the very beginning.

The Author

A braham Jones is an international motivational speaker, a counsellor, spiritual teacher, relationship expert, and a business and recruitment consultant. Abraham Jones speaks at conferences, seminars and various conventions across the world. The central theme of his message is focused on raising living epistles and intrinsically repositioning people in order for them to find true fulfilment in life.

He is the coordinator of the Life Singles Network and Kingdom Relationships, bodies that are aimed at equipping singles, strengthening relationships and marriages via conferences, seminars and workshops across the United Kingdom and across the world.

Abraham is the author of *True Fulfillment*, a book that has helped many people discover themselves and find true fulfilment in life. He is the host of a weekly program "Kingdom Relationships" aired on radio stations across the UK. He has earned degrees from American Liberty University and London Business College. He studied Christian leadership in Bible school.

Abraham Jones resides in London, England, with his lovely wife Ashma. They are blessed with a precious son, Joshua Jones.

For more information about the author, visit:-

www.abrahamjones.com

www.lifesinglesnetwork.com

www.kingdomrelationships.com

Made in the USA
Charleston, SC
09 May 2016